THE KINDNESS REVOLUTION

THE KINDNESS
REVOLUTION

The Company-Wide Culture Shift
That Inspires Phenomenal Customer Service

ED HORRELL

⁙AMACOM

AMERICAN MANAGEMENT ASSOCIATION

New York • Atlanta • Brussels • Chicago • Mexico City • San Francisco
Shanghai • Tokyo • Toronto • Washington, D.C.

Special discounts on bulk quantities of AMACOM books are available to corporations, professional associations, and other organizations. For details, contact Special Sales Department, AMACOM, a division of American Management Association, 1601 Broadway, New York, NY 10019.
Tel.: 212-903-8316.   Fax: 212-903-8083.
Website: www.amacombooks.org

This publication is designed to provide accurate and authoritative information in regard to the subject matter covered. It is sold with the understanding that the publisher is not engaged in rendering legal, accounting, or other professional service. If legal advice or other expert assistance is required, the services of a competent professional person should be sought.

Library of Congress Cataloging-in-Publication Data

Horrell, Edward.
    The kindness revolution : the company-wide culture shift that inspires phenomenal customer service / Ed Horrell.
        p.   cm.
    Includes index.
    ISBN-10: 0-8144-7307-5 (hardcover)
    ISBN-13: 978-0-8144-7307-8 (hardcover)
    1. Customer relations.   2. Industrial relations.   I. Title.

HF5415.5.K537 2006
658.8′12—dc22

                                                    2006007483

Printing number

10   9   8   7   6   5   4   3

To the kindness of two of their generation's greatest . . .
my Mom and Dad.

CONTENTS

PREFACE

THIS BOOK TRACES a quest that I began during the summer of 2004 to find examples of top service providers. I am pleased with what I discovered about certain companies that are known for their customer service excellence, and eager to share my conclusions as to what other companies must do in order to provide this excellence.

To gather my information and make my findings, I personally contacted and interviewed representatives from many of the companies I chronicle. For others, I relied on the experiences of friends and family as well as book and Internet research to verify what I had been told.

I am deeply appreciative for all who have made contributions to this book. The names are far too numerous to mention, as they include contributors who simply made suggestions or called my radio talk show, *Talk About Service,* and mentioned either a company name or an experience regarding service. These stories and comments are what led me to my findings and conclusions.

Readers should be forewarned that I am a staunch customer service advocate and that I am constantly fighting for improvement in service. That said, I am also something of a customer service skeptic these days as I am constantly dismayed by what so many companies are offering in the name of service, while being completely clueless as to what their customers think of that service.

Consider these e-mail segments, sent to me by one of my listeners concerning her service issues with one of the best-known wireless companies in America:

> *My inquiry:* How come I am being charged for calls in my calling area, incoming calls, and calls that are made on nights and weekends?

> *Their response:* Ma'am, your plan doesn't cover Tennessee. It covers Iowa and parts of western Arkansas.

> *Me:* OK, Sir, I don't know if you're looking at your screen there, but I live in Tennessee. I've always lived in Tennessee. I've never been to Iowa or western Arkansas and, basically you're wrong.

And this exchange with the same company:

> *My inquiry:* I changed my address on a form on the back of your bill months ago, but am still getting mail forwarded from my old address. What's the problem?

> *Them:* Ma'am, sometimes, you have to call and tell us. We're more likely to get the address change that way. Sometimes they don't even look on the back.

> *Me:* But, wait a minute. Your company makes the process. I followed your process, right?

> *Them:* Yes, Ma'am, but sometimes it's better if you just call instead.

Me: OK, well, it seems to me that's what I am presently doing. Do you think there is any way you can assist me instead of annoying me?

Them: Yes, Ma'am, I will put in your request. Is there anything else I can help you with?

Me: Yes, can you tell me the soonest date when I can cancel my plan?

Them: December 10th. (Note: They did not try to talk me out of this—she could have cared less.)

The listeners of my talk show send me this type of correspondence literally every day. Sometimes it seems that there is a certain satisfaction on the part of some customers to find the very worst example of service that they can, especially when they have personally experienced it. In any case, service levels are discussed *constantly*, and yet what fascinates me is that so many companies continue to be oblivious to what their customers are thinking and saying about their service!

This disconnect between what complacent companies are providing in the name of service and what their customers are saying about them is intriguing. Just as intriguing to me is what the companies that provide "legendary" service have in common. This became the journey for me: to discover what the great service providers have in common. You'll see that this is not simply another book about customer service; you won't find a lot of "answer calls on the second ring" or "get back to your customers quickly." It *is* a book about what *every* company must focus on to provide compassionate service. Not *systems* to provide it, but rather the ingredients that make it literally impossible *not* to provide it. These are principles that any company can follow, regardless of industry, location, or size.

Numerous surveys indicate that the biggest reason that companies lose customers is an attitude of "indifference" on the part of one employee. A single employee can be the reason that you lose a customer for life. It's important for companies to understand that such an employee is not necessarily in management. Donald Trump has been quoted as saying that one of the most important ingredients to success in business is the attitude of the valet who parks the cars at a fine restaurant, the bag boy at a country club, or the bellman who greets patrons at hotels. He says that this can be what makes or breaks a quality experience at the venue.

During this quest, it became clear to me that there was something that drove certain companies to provide exceptional and compassionate customer service. Many were clearly head and shoulders above the others. They include L.L.Bean, Chick-fil-A, Nordstrom, Mrs. Fields, St. Jude Children's Research Center, The Ritz-Carlton, FedEx, and an outsource company to FedEx— the inspiring Baddour Center, which is staffed by mentally challenged adults and creates complex welcome packages that FedEx uses to greet its customers for the first time. While each is different in its own right—retail, fast-food, service, not for profit, some public, some private—they all share certain qualities.

Each of these companies is driven by a distinct, clearly visible value system that permeates the entire organization. Not coincidentally, these values were introduced into each company by its founder. Similarly, I discovered that each of these firms also understands, and practices, the value of kindness, in their dealings with employees as well as customers. Kindness appears to be a key, if not *the* key, in companies that "own" their customers rather than "renting" them.

Throughout the book, we will see that ownership of customers does not come as a result of technology, techniques, or organization. Ownership of customers—actually having customers who are going to do business with you regardless of your location, price, or competition—comes as a result of values at the core of the company. I'll share with you my theory about "the onion effect": what happens when the layers of a company are peeled back to expose the beliefs that appear at the core.

You'll find herein very clear distinctions among some companies as to the ways in which they do business. These qualities lead to some companies having a different type of workplace, a different type of employee, and even a different type of customer—a "more fun" workplace, more dedicated employees, and more loyal customers.

STANDARDS AND CHALLENGES

Each of the companies that I portray here has set the bar for a standard that becomes the model for others. They also offer a challenge for any company that desires to emulate the excellence they portray. In this book, I will identify the challenges that you'll face as you work toward emulating these companies.

I will also note examples of excellence displayed by a few companies other than the ones covered in more detail. While they may not be included among the standard bearers to which I refer, they are setting examples by which all companies of excellence should be measured.

The Kindness Revolution began as the journal of my discovery of the best, but distinctly different, service providers—some of which are household names—and what they all have in common that allows them to eliminate indifference throughout their workplace and organization. I hope these stories will both educate and inspire you. At the least, this book should provide valuable lessons for companies of all sizes in their quest to eliminate indifference in their workplace. If you apply what you learn from this book to your own organization, I think you'll find the results interesting and motivating for you and your firm. You can re-energize your company's customer service and inspire greater customer loyalty by launching a company-wide culture shift—a Kindness Revolution of your own.

MY QUEST FOR THE BEST

I AM A PROFESSIONAL SPEAKER, freelance writer, author, and radio talk show host. I actually launched my radio show, *Talk About Service*, after I began the original research for this book, but that role has helped me enormously by constantly validating what I found on this quest for customer service excellence. The exposure to listeners via both telephone calls and e-mails has supported the information I will be presenting to you. All of the stories, quotes, and e-mails are real and reflect the current state of customer service from actual customers with whom I have come into contact. You won't have to look very closely to determine my overall opinion of service today.

As a customer service advocate, I figured it was about time to write a book on the topic, a book chronicling some of the companies that have become famous for their outstanding customer service. Being from the South (Memphis, Tennessee), I was interested in exploring whether being southern-based made a difference in customer service. I finally decided that that approach was too limited, so I came up with a combination of national and regional companies.

PROBLEMS GETTING THE RIGHT INFORMATION

The initial contacts went pretty well. Interviews were scheduled and being conducted. I was feeling pretty good at that point, but problems developed fairly early. I found that the first couple of companies I interviewed wanted to emphasize what I can only describe as "extreme" customer service stories. I felt that the people I was interviewing were more interested in telling amazing, almost unbelievable, stories than talking about their customer service philosophies.

I had explained that what I wanted were the stories from which other companies could learn how to improve their service. But the stories I got did not contain examples of customer service from which others could learn; they were more about heroic acts performed by employees. They included life-saving experiences and stories of babies being delivered by company employees. I enjoyed hearing the stories but felt that these tended to center around people doing nice things rather than around customer service. I would hope that we live in a society where human decency is a common trait, but these were not customer service-related stories. Frankly, I expect any company anywhere to help a stranger who has a seizure in their restaurant or lobby.

What I was sensing was an extreme disconnect between what customers expect and what these companies thought of as good service. It appeared that many of the companies I was interviewing didn't really grasp what their customers wanted. They wanted to talk about heroic acts but not their regular, everyday customer service. After a quick review of what could have been my faulty interviewing techniques, I moved on.

I was then told by executives at two companies that they had excellent stories, but they were hesitant to share them because their customers might read the book and would then expect the same service.

You didn't misread that last sentence. They didn't want to tell me their customer service excellence stories because they didn't want their other customers to expect that level of service! This shocked me and left me disappointed. The stories they didn't want to tell me were not about incredible acts of bravery or courage, but simply about superior acts of service. In both cases, the message was "We don't want our customers to know what we are capable of doing because they would come to expect that." They would rather have their customers expect mediocrity because they knew they could deliver that. This was unbelievable to me.

I also had my share of stories from founders of companies who thought that their individual "rags to riches" stories were bookworthy, but whose companies just didn't seem to have the passion for service that I was looking for. These were nice companies, but I found that something was lacking from a sense-of-service standpoint. While their individual stories would be of interest to readers, the resulting commitments to service didn't provide what I was looking for either.

By now, I had interviewed a few companies with interesting stories, but I wasn't finding the synergies that I had expected. As a matter of fact, I was finding virtually nothing in common among the companies I was interviewing. They were all successful businesses in their industries, but none was providing any kind of "wow" when it came to service. I found that I had selected them more because I knew who they were than for their reputation among their customers or the buying populace in general. In other words, I had selected them based upon their marketing—their advertising and slogans—not their service. I had selected them based on what *they* said about their service, not what their *customers* said.

I realized that I had to change my approach and change it soon. I had run my mouth to friends and associates about my new book and was too far into it to simply stop, although I had gotten almost nowhere. My notes were worthless and had no meaning. I was committed to avoiding writing another customer service book containing a collection of processes or tips for dealing with angry customers and the like. I knew full well that I wasn't going to go with quantifiable data-type information simply because that is neither my style nor interest. I wanted to be inspired, to find some driving force behind service that was more than zero defects and systems.

I decided to make a list of the companies that I did business with. I wanted to determine which of these companies I would never consider leaving as opposed to those that I would leave if I got better service somewhere else. I needed to know whether I was an example of a customer surrounded by effective service. I got out a sheet of paper and began to write them down, all of them.

With one or two exceptions, I found that I wouldn't hesitate to leave any of them to do business with another company that gave me better service. This was in spite of the fact that I had done business with some of these companies for over twenty years! I was not a loyal customer and probably was not even satisfied. A better description would be that I was mostly not *dissatisfied*. Most of them simply offered routine service and a comfort that came simply by knowing their location and phone numbers. There was nothing that compelled me to continue to do business with them other than the fact that I had done business with them for a long time. Not loyal, not satisfied; I was simply complacent.

THE IMPORTANCE OF WOW!

I recently spoke at a hotel management company annual conference. The theme of their conference was "The Future Is Wow!" That theme has a lot of possible connotations, including a better future, more profits, and exciting new ideas. In my presentation, I applied it to customer service in the sense that the future of companies that make a difference in customer service had better include "WOW" for their customers. Satisfaction is not going to be enough for the ones who wish to enjoy extreme success. It is going to require that they do more than satisfy . . . they are going to have to astonish, amaze, and "WOW" their customers.

Sooner or later, a group of companies will realize that service is what makes the difference. They are going to decide to win back the lost customer loyalty that once prevailed among customers and get them back by killing them with service. They are going to quit talking about it, put away the fads and trends, and get down to the old-fashioned business of providing world-class customer service. They are going to get their old customers back, and also the customers of their competition. The others, the companies who fail to "WOW" their customers, are going to have problems. Indeed, the future for all companies is "WOW." Failure to provide that will result in failure.

SOME COMPANIES GET IT; SOME DON'T

During my speech, I introduced one of my favorite theories in customer service. It is the theory that there are two types of companies when it comes to service: those that "get it," and those that don't.

One of my favorite companies that "get it" is The Ritz-Carlton. The stories of the Ritz-Carlton mystique are legendary. That mystique comes not from legend, but from a relentless quest to astonish their guests. They understand at The Ritz-Carlton that any hotel can provide guest satisfaction; that doesn't create mystique. What they want is to amaze their guests, at every guest contact, to the extent that comparisons with other hotels are meaningless.

That is astonishment; being incomparable. That is "WOW."

As a full-time observer of customer service, I pay attention to companies' media ads. I like to see what gets customers' attention and to try to compare what companies *say* about service, rather than what they actually *do*. One of my favorite ads was sent to me by a listener. It was an ad for a local mattress dealer. It said, "If you can find a mattress for less than you can buy it for here, we'll give you one free." I love that—it's simple and direct and shows both confidence in their pricing and respect for their customers. It's also another clear-cut example of "WOW"—even though the company isn't anywhere near as large or well-known as The Ritz-Carlton,

In fact, I notice that the most passionate ads about service and commitment often come from the smaller companies. When it comes to customer service, size is not necessarily an advantage. What matters is whether you "get it" or not.

THE REASON YOU ARE IN BUSINESS

I enjoy watching new companies get started. I am an entrepreneur and certainly consider myself a small-business advocate. I like to see the growth of new business; I take pleasure in observing the passion of a new business owner. I believe the opportunities for new businesses to be a blessing that comes with living in the United States.

Most new businesses begin as a result of an observation that there is a service or product needed to fill a niche. This niche can be a void in a location, a need for a new or enhanced product, the development of a similar product or service at a lower price, or any number of similar observations. In all events, the observer has determined that money can be made through these efforts. Often, this comes as a result of a detailed study of the market, prospects, competition, and other factors. Just as often, it comes as a result of a gut feeling. Either way, the business begins.

During the course of time, some of these businesses begin to separate themselves from their competition; they develop a sense and mission that become apparent to their customers and employees. These become clearer and more apparent; they have a purpose and course. Their turnover goes down, and profits go up. Their customers are happy, and their employees become empowered and more trusted. They become model companies, often recognized as leaders and innovators in their industries. There is something special and different about them, something that is sensed, but not measured.

The principals of these companies become well-known and are asked regularly to speak or to be interviewed for the next article. They are asked to describe why they are in business. Amazingly, the answer is virtually always the same: "to make money."

This tends to surprise a lot of people. I often ask my audiences to describe why these leading companies are in business, and I get a kick out of the many times that I hear "to make a difference," "to provide great service," "to serve their customers," or something similar. The correct answer, however, is "to make money."

The companies that "get it" when it comes to service understand that making money comes directly as a result of serving customers. They put the focus on the service part of business and realize that money flows from loyal customers. They understand a simple equation: Having loyal customers equals making money.

What really is surprising, however, is the number of companies that view service as the item to *cut* in order to make more money. They decide to focus on getting new customers at the expense of keeping existing customers loyal. When things get tough, they look at ways to cut the costs associated with service. They look for ways to cut back on employee costs but keep the heat up on finding new customers. They lose sight of the fact that it usually costs around five times as much to acquire a new customer as it does to keep an existing one. These are the companies that just don't get it.

DOES YOUR COMPANY GET IT?

If you have to wonder whether your company gets it when it comes to customer service, it probably doesn't. However, you might take this quick assessment and answer the following five questions honestly:

1. *Does your company have a mission statement posted in the lobby or conference room that is known by memory by no one in your firm and never referred to?* Do you have a nicely framed lithograph on the wall in your lobby, with no purpose but to fill up space?

2. *Do you discuss customer service less than once a day with your direct reports?* Do your customer service initiatives consist only of having a speaker come in during your annual sales meeting?

3. *Would you be embarrassed or ashamed of what you think your employees say about you and your company after hours?* Are your employees poor advertisers and recruiters—or worse—after hours?

4. *Are you hesitant to tell your employees to do whatever it takes to make a customer happy . . . whatever it takes?* Are you concerned that they would "give away the ship" if you let them?

5. *Do you think you know what your customers want without asking them?* Are you comfortable sitting in the conference room making decisions on behalf of your customers?

"Yes" answers to any of these questions may mean trouble—for you, your customers, your employees, and, above all, your company.

TOO MANY COMPANIES DON'T GET IT

I asked the president of a local technology company about his thoughts on customer service. His response disappointed me. He immediately started bragging about his operating system, the cost of the software that had been installed, and all that it did from a management perspective. He went on and on about the information that he and his staff could get on the flow of orders, trouble reports, and status of trouble tickets. At no time did he mention his people. His answers all involved the process that his company took in dealing with customers; things like reports, systems, and details. What was important to him was the software that ran the system, not the people who ran the software.

This executive thinks he is running a good company, and he is. His problem is that he is running a company based upon what his competition does. They drive his organization, his vision. He runs a company that is just another business on the block, not unique in any way. He is doing business to find satisfied customers and not to create loyalty. His company is just another player in the game, not one that "gets it."

Unfortunately, this is all too typical of most of the companies that are viewed as successful today. They are happy with middle-of-the-road success, with mediocrity. What they don't realize is that there is a company that gets it that is waiting in the wings, watching their complacency closely. These observers know their customers, their employees, and their methods. They are just like everyone else, so why shouldn't they be known? So, the first company continues to plug ahead, until the other company makes itself known—the one doing business with values at its core; the one that changes things for the entire industry.

THE SILVER RULE OF CUSTOMER SERVICE

One of the premises I teach regarding interpersonal communication is that the Golden Rule (*Do unto others as you would have others do unto you*), though infallible as a way of life, does not work when it comes to effective communication. We should seek to communicate with others not the way *we* wish to be communicated with, but rather the way *they* wish to be communicated with—what I call the "Silver Rule of Customer Service."

Behavior has been observed since ancient times, and theories as to why people behave as they do are boundless. What all behavioral studies support, however, is that different people like to be treated differently. Not everyone wants to be treated the same—whether employee or customer, one size does not fit all. The companies that "get it" know that different behavioral styles are to be celebrated, not resented. The result is that they treat each customer with respect in spite of the fact that he or she might behave or do things differently.

This acceptance and celebration of people's differences leads to effective teamwork. The respect for the other team players grows and permeates through the organization to the customers. As I was to later discover, this process was to be identified and would explain the differences among many companies and their customers.

TAKING INVENTORY OF YOUR PEOPLE

One of the popular business clichés is "Our people are our assets." This has been worn out from misuse, but it is true. People are assets. This is especially true for the companies that get it, but not true for the others. In their case, employees are their liabilities.

It is imperative that you determine whether or not your employees are assets or liabilities. Just like the value of your products, goods, or service, you should regularly take an inventory of your employees. While this can begin with performance reviews, it is more than that and much more important. It consists of determining what each employee brings to the organization from a standpoint different from a particular skill set.

The inventory to which I am referring is an inventory of each employee with regard to his or her values and attitudes as they compare with those at the core of your company. It assesses not so much the value of an employee but rather the "fit" within your company. It consists of simple yes/no questions that should be asked of every person in your firm, top to bottom. Try it for yourself on your employees.

- Does this employee make me proud that he or she works in my company?

- Would I trust the keys of the company to this employee?

- Would I be proud if I knew what this employee said about my company after work?

- Would I be pleased if I had an entire company made up of employees like this one?

- Is this employee thoughtful around other employees?

- Is this employee respectful around people of different races, genders, cultures, and ages?

- Is this employee honest?

If you didn't answer "Yes" to every question here, you have some problems. Also note that nowhere did I ask about the *skills* of your employees. Those can be taught.

I recently met with the president of a large plumbing company in Atlanta called Superior Plumbing. It has a reputation for quality, integrity, and honesty, even to the extent of using the tagline "the Honest Plumber." The CEO told me the story of the way the company recruits and selects new hires. He explained to me that because it "put it on the line" in stating that it was honest, it had no choice but to hire people of character. It didn't require experience in the industry. What it did require was character, someone whom customers would feel comfortable having in their homes.

I strongly believe that good customer service starts with people, not process. If you hire people with good attitudes, they will be good employees and, in turn, will attract good customers. Some of the world-class providers of service have determined that skills can be taught much more easily than attitudes. The practice of hiring character and teaching skills works for the best, so it will work for you.

CHAPTER ONE

OWNING YOUR CUSTOMERS

"It has become appallingly obvious that our technology has exceeded our humanity."
—ALBERT EINSTEIN

ASK MOST CONSUMERS and businesses today, and they will tell you that customer service is at an all-time low. I, myself, am sick and tired of the service I get from most companies these days.

What I do find, and find often, is that there are customers who wouldn't dream of doing business with anyone but a few selected companies. In spite of location, higher prices, and competition, these customers talk about their good experiences with these service providers, and they go back to these companies time and time again.

I call this "owning" your customer. Most companies simply "rent" their customers, by which I mean that their customers are loyal to them until another company comes along that offers the same product or service, but with a different style, a different manner, a different kind of customer service.

Companies in the same field essentially all do the same things as their competitors! They have procedures they follow and steps to take to do business. This is their process; this is their job. It is *how* they *do* this job that separates them. Some companies simply go about their job in an efficient manner and compete for customers like everybody else in their industry. These companies aim for customer satisfaction, but satisfied customers are not loyal, they are simply lingering. But some companies want to offer a higher level of service. Their goal is to astonish, amaze, or overwhelm their customers. These are the companies that "own" their customers.

THEY'RE NOT ALL HAPPY

Before we go too far, let me restate the obvious fact that we don't live in a sea of deliriously happy customers. During the interviews I conducted for this book, it was much easier to get the terrible stories than the good ones! It seems that people like to tell the bad stories, but not with nearly the passion as when they tell the good ones. (I do, however, have to mention the story of kindness that one elderly lady told me about a BellSouth operator who called an ambulance and stayed on the line with her when she had fallen and broken her hip. She swore that she was alive today because of that one call. I wouldn't want to be the telemarketing rep with a BellSouth competitor when they call to solicit *her* business!) But the bad stories that were told to me surpassed the good stories by at least three to one! People *love* to talk about their bad customer service experiences, and if you treat them indifferently, they will love to talk about *your* company.

The companies I discovered while writing this book all have one thing in common . . . a common thread that runs deep through the soul of the company. The thread is invisible, but measurable. It is detectable. Customer service icon Tom Peters has compared outstanding customer service to the aroma of bread baking in the oven. What he means is that it can be sensed as soon as you walk in the door or have someone answer the telephone at a company that provides exceptional customer service. I have indeed sensed this feeling. I have come to the conclusion that this feeling, this "aroma of bread baking," represents the values of the companies we'll discuss. I have observed that wonderful things happen when values replace indifference in customer service.

What values am I taking about here? They're simple:

- Dignity

- Respect

- Courtesy

- Kindness

The companies that own their customers practice these values from top to bottom in their organizations. These values are a part of their culture, engrained in the company. They have learned somewhere, somehow, one of the most valuable lessons of customer service that exists today. That lesson is this: The way you treat your employees will be the way they treat your customers. I have found this to be a universal truth; it never fails.

During my quest for top service providers, I also noticed another attribute that is common to the companies who own their customers. It is true of all the companies that provide excellence in service. It is as if they have all read the same book, read the same manual, watched the same videos. They practice *kindness* in dealing with both employees and customers.

BEING IN TOUCH WITH CUSTOMERS

First of all, and perhaps most important, the companies that own their customers know what it is that their customers want! This sounds so easy, but I found that very few companies actually practice it. Most companies *think* they know what their customers want, and are too happy to give it to their customers, even to the extent of forcing it down their customers' throats. This attitude resonates in companies with which you do business today. Now that you are made aware of this, look around and notice how often you see it.

Let's look at the banking industry as an example. Most banks now push their "free checking accounts." Good idea . . . free is always good. Most people will take two if they're free.

However, go back to the core values I listed above . . . dignity, respect, courtesy, and kindness. Now, give me a bank that dishes that combo out to me each time I visit the teller or manager. A sincere greeting when I get to the front of the line. Maybe an occasional "How are your boys?" or "Try to stay warm today . . . it's going to get cold later." I'm there a lot; this is not a difficult task. Something that says there is an actual person on the other side at the drive-thru teller. And if an occasionally lonely person needs to talk a minute longer, so be it.

Now, after I've been experiencing that treatment for a while, after the bank employees have been doling out the dignity, respect, courtesy, and kindness, let someone else try to get my business. No way. My bank would own me. I'll spend the extra few minutes going past another bank to get to mine. I'll even pay a little for my checking account. But most banks don't want to go to the trouble of offering that kind of service. They don't need to. They think they know what we want—indifference and free checking. To most of them, we're not customers, we're accounts.

It's the same way most restaurants know what we want . . . good, quick food served with indifference. Same with hotels; we want quick registration with a little indifference. Doctor's clinics know it. Add in law firms, dental practices, government offices, automobile service locations, retail shops, maintenance companies, and grocery stores. Get 'em in, get 'em out, watch the bottom line, and the customer will be okay.

And they're right, everything else being equal. Customers will be okay until they find the service provider who gives the same good quality with kindness. Then they're gone. Adios. Vamoose. History. The companies that don't know this merely rent their customers.

AN EXAMPLE OF OWNING CUSTOMERS

One of my clients is a software distributor. It is very good at what it does and constantly strives to improve its service to its clients. It wants to improve and is not reluctant to spend money to improve its already excellent service. My introduction to it came as a result of a change in technology that it was prepared to implement to improve its customer service. Part of the planned change was a conversion to an automated answering service as part of its telephone system. It had observed the calling patterns of its clients and had determined that the automated system would be an asset to them and that the system would improve efficiency while reducing costs. The system had been identified, and the company was ready to purchase it.

Company executives contacted me about helping to train their client contact reps in overall customer service communication as part of the upgrade. Their concern was getting their employees ready for implementation. During the course of our meetings, I asked whether they had contacted their customers, seeking feedback about the proposed changes. Surprisingly, they admitted that they had not.

Let me point out that these principals are not typical of the type who think they know what their customers want. These guys are passionate about their service and were pleased to ask their clients what they desired. They immediately grasped the concept of a client survey and were enthusiastic about what they would learn, as opposed to being fearful of learning what their customer base thought of them.

The results were interesting if not surprising. The overwhelming majority of their clients did not want the new service, and it was scrapped. What was even more interesting was the positive response from the anonymous survey, which reflected significant client appreciation at being asked before implementing the changes.

The company then took advantage of what was a terrific marketing opportunity. It conducted a focus group, shared the responses with the complete customer base, implemented a new set of customer service basics to its staff, developed a new logo and website, and virtually reinvented itself with much success—most of it due to its quest to be better than it had been. It also implemented a software tracking system by which it now measures (and rewards) its improved response times to customer problems. It knows, day-by-day, exactly how it is doing with its process and has put relentless emphasis on its people skills as well. By going outside its boardroom to ask what could make it better, it discovered it—by asking its customers what was needed, as opposed to thinking it simply knew it all the time.

Great customer service comes only as the result of great customer knowledge. The companies that "get it" understand that customer desires are not determined in the boardroom. They are not decided on how *we* want to be served. They are decided when we ask our customers how they want to be treated.

YOU HAVE TO ASK CUSTOMERS WHAT THEY WANT

There are a number of ways to get the feedback from your customers that will cause you to serve them they way they want to be served. It is not my intention here to discuss how this feedback is best collected, but rather to impress the importance of going to the trouble to get it. Whether it is surveys, feedback forms, focus groups, or individual meetings with clients, the point is to listen to what your customers are saying and give them what they want!

You'll find that most of your customers will be extremely candid and helpful in their feedback about your company. Customers gain absolutely no benefit in being hesitant to provide feedback. What they might be hesitant to do, however, is to spend an inordinate amount of time responding to surveys. So, make sure that you remember the importance of time when surveying your customers. Be brief, and be specific.

Also, you can expect a greater response with anonymous surveys. In the example above, my client used a combination of anonymous surveys along with a smaller focus group to confirm what was discovered in the first survey. This combination worked very well and led to significant improvement in service levels.

PRACTICING EXTREME CUSTOMER SERVICE

Customer service comes in three flavors, but most companies understand only two. The first of these is dissatisfaction. This one is easy. This occurs when your customers are simply not happy. They are displeased. They don't like the treatment they're getting. We are not talking about the quality of the product; we are talking about the quality of the service that they have received during either the purchase process or a follow-up after a problem has occurred.

One of the "disconnects" that I found within companies is the failure to understand the difference between satisfaction and the lack of dissatisfaction. Lack of dissatisfaction is apathy; I'm not satisfied, I'm simply there.

The second flavor is satisfaction. This occurs when customers are okay with their service provider, but not "wowed." This is where problems begin in a quest for excellence, since customer satisfaction is too often the goal of companies. Again, this is a major "disconnect" since satisfaction should not be the goal. Satisfaction should be the norm, to be expected.

The third flavor should be your quest. This is customer loyalty, creating a customer who is going to stay with you (again, we'll be referring to this as "owning" your customer). Oftentimes, owning your customer will require radical change in the way you do business, but the results will be radical as well. Unfortunately, the effort is not for the faint of heart.

THE RELENTLESS PURSUIT

In June 2001 there was an article in *Fast Company* magazine about a company called EMC ("Customer Service: EMC Corp.," by Paul C. Judge). It's not a household name; you've never heard of it unless you're in the information technology business. You'll remember it after you hear this story.

In 1988, its operations executive, Mike Ruettgers, found himself traveling the country and apologizing to the company's customers for poor performance. Things weren't good, either for the company or its customers. The company had sent faulty products to its customers, and the customers weren't happy, to say the least. According to *Fast Company* magazine, Ruettgers was an "executive punching bag," traveling from customer to customer apologizing for EMC's problems. He felt he had hit bottom when he met with a customer who broke down and cried as he related that he would probably lose his job as a result of the EMC problems.

As a result of his travels, Ruettgers took a radical step. He offered his unhappy customers a choice. They could either choose to take a replacement product manufactured by EMC or take a comparable product manufactured by their leading competitor, IBM, and paid for by EMC. Yes, you read that correctly. During one quarter of 1989, EMC actually shipped more IBM products than it did its own!

Focusing on improvement of its own product, EMC found that many customers were willing to give it another chance due to its relentless quest for quality, its "fanatical devotion" to service. It was coming back, and coming back in droves. According to Ruettgers, "What that proved to me, to all of us, was that when a customer believes in you, and you go to great lengths to preserve that relationship, they'll stick with you almost no matter what. It opened our eyes to the power of customer service."

Does it work? Let's see. In 1988, EMC had annual sales of $123 million, 910 employees, and losses of $7.8 million. In 2004, annual sales were over $8 billion, it had over 20,000 employees, and profits were over $830 million.

By the way, Michael Ruettgers is now the chairman of the board of EMC.

BEWARE COMPLACENCY AND ARROGANCE

I want to point out that success via values and focus on service should be a never-ending quest. The "best" do not cease in their efforts. They constantly grow through their relentless focus on those values that made them successful. They remember who they are and how they got there, never falling prey to arrogance or complacency. While there are stories of short-term success as a result of radical customer service changes, the true leaders continue their success in a manner consistent with their values. When the focus is constantly on values, employees, and customers, success is virtually guaranteed. We'll see later why the Laws of the Universe promise that.

There are three equations I often use in regard to success in business. They follow in order and lead to the third one. They are as follows:

1. *Poor quality leads to ultimate failure.* It makes no difference how you serve it up. Poor quality equals failure.

2. *Good quality with indifference* can *equal success.* People will tolerate indifference for an outstanding product or service. (Do you remember the classic "Soup Nazi" episode of *Seinfeld*? This episode was based on a real soup store in New York, where the proprietor was known for his rude "order-and-get-out" attitude toward his patrons, but the place was wildly successful because the soup was so good.)

3. *Quality plus kindness equals ownership.* What the Soup Nazi doesn't realize is that he is just renting his customers until someone opens across the street with the same quality soup served with kindness. His customers will be gone. The shop across the street will own them.

I know that some of you reading this now are rolling your eyes! You are thinking to yourself, "This guy has got to be kidding! Business is about bottom lines, about management. It is inventory management and gross margins. Quality is measurable. I know how to determine quality . . . I learned it during my MBA training."

I find these cynics in my audiences sometimes and can spot them easily. They get uneasy when I talk about how values, courtesy, and kindness can make a difference in business. They haven't been taught that, and they don't like it! They sit there with furrowed brows, arms folded across their chests. To them, and to any who may be feeling that way as you read this, I say this: If you don't believe that eliminating indifference with your customers is one of your first priorities, please send me your address. I want to rent the place next door to you and open a business just like yours. I am going to do two things: I am going to get your employees, and I'm going to get your customers.

ATTITUDE VS. SKILL

I conducted an informal survey a few months ago. I asked friends and colleagues in academia what was being taught in school, especially in higher education. The results, very broadly stated, were that students were being taught "how to," such as "how to be an engineer," "how to be a doctor," (or an attorney or a teacher, etc.).

In fact, the general consensus was that about 90 percent of what students were being taught was "how to." Those being surveyed went further to say that only about 10 percent of what students were learning dealt with attitudes, and that the vast majority of that learning came from extracurricular activities, such as fine arts, band, or athletics.

I then asked a similar question to a number of business owners, CEOs, and senior managers, "What attributes are most important in employees today?" Their answer: "Attitude is by far the most important attribute in employees; the "how to" is easily learned."

A NICE CUP OF INDIFFERENCE

My fiancée and I were awaiting a flight recently in the Memphis airport. She suggested that we stop and have a cup of coffee at the coffee shop near the gate.

This coffee shop has become a household name around the

country. It is known for the various flavors and sizes of the coffees that come with grandiose names . . . and pretty Grande prices. We stood in line behind an elderly lady and patiently waited to get to the front of the line. The lady who was serving the coffee was obviously interested in moving the line along as quickly as possible. Courtesy was not her priority that day, forward motion was.

As we neared the front of the line, the elderly lady ahead of us put her finger up against the glass pane behind which were the pastries for sale. She kindly said, "I'll have this sweet roll," while pointing directly to the desired item.

"We don't have any sweet rolls," snapped the counter person.

The lady was obviously both flustered and nervous, what with the crowd accumulating behind her impatiently. "What is this, then?" she asked.

"It's a Danish," was the curt reply.

Somewhat embarrassed by the whole thing, the lady reached in her purse, paid for her coffee, and moved on. My question was "What did she do to deserve this harsh treatment in the first place?" What if she had said, "I'll have this rolled up piece of dough covered with sugar and this artificial fruit stuff in the middle"? I would have preferred that the server respond with something like, "Good choice. I think you'll enjoy it with your coffee." Couldn't she have been treated with a little kindness, a little dignity?

No, she got an expensive cup of coffee with a splash of indifference. The coffee shop lost an additional sale, however small it may have been. And the chain lost one customer for good . . . me.

WHAT MAKES THE DIFFERENCE?

As I began to question associates, family, friends, and clients, I wanted to know which companies provided the finest in customer service. I quickly modified my question to include, "What do they do differently?"

The answer began to surface immediately. It was almost always some variation of "They are nice."

Now this created a problem for me. I didn't want to accept this. I couldn't write a book with this as its premise. I wanted something more measurable, more quantifiable.

The more I looked, however, it became clearer and clearer. Outstanding service is not a process. It is not the elimination of problems or defects. It *is* the style with which companies perform their process and deal with customer problems. It is not perfection, but the relentless pursuit of customer service, wrapped in values.

I found that the companies that do their jobs and add values to their process will own their customers. Others keep their customers until their customers experience service provided by competitive companies with values. The customers then will leave for the company with values.

For now, let me say that value-based customer service is easily detected when we learn what to look for. Early in my quest, I didn't know what that was. I *did* know that I had developed some questions I wanted answered. For example:

- *Why are some companies so committed to customer satisfaction?*

- *Why do some companies give employees leeway in making decisions?*

- *Why do some employees love their jobs?*

- *How do some companies keep customer service at the top of their employees' minds?*

- *Can work really be fun?*

- *Do the values at the top of companies mean anything?*

- *What's the best way to hire the "right" employees?*

I found the answers to all these questions . . . and more.

INDIFFERENCE IS THE SERVICE KILLER

For years, the American Society for Quality has stated the importance that indifference plays in customer service. Numerous surveys have indicated that the number-one reason that customers vow never to return to a specific place of service is due to an attitude of indifference on the part of one employee. I ask this question in every survey I perform for my clients, and it is validated in every instance.

Companies that own their customers understand who their company is to their customer. It is not the executives, management, or owners. It is not the advertising or public relations campaign. It is not the mission statement. It is the person in direct contact with the customer: the receptionist, the wait staff, the technician. That person *is* the company.

I recently had a terrible experience with a major airline carrier. I was supposed to travel to Pittsburgh to give a talk. After boarding, the passengers discovered that we had to get off the plane, and the flight was subsequently cancelled.

As chaos reigned, I was called by an attendant to the gate to discuss how to get a later flight. It was toward the end of the regular work day, and the staff members were obviously more interested in getting to their after-work destinations than in getting me to Pittsburgh! When they discovered that they couldn't make the necessary change in my ticket, they had to call their supervisor.

My next flight was going to leave soon, so I was in a hurry. I politely asked how long this might take, as it was getting close to departure, and they called their supervisor to get her to speed up a little. I was told, "Here she comes now." I looked up to see a lady strolling toward the gate laughing and talking with another lady. When I say *strolling*, I mean *strolling*. Not an ounce of urgency or service to help her customer, just a casual stroll through the airport.

I was treated with indifference, and I didn't like it. I barely made my flight, but I did get to Pittsburgh in time to deliver my speech. Needless to say, I told my audience about my experience and the indifference in my service.

However, it actually got worse. Upon arriving back in Memphis, I went to the luggage ramp that was identified in the terminal. After some time, I went to the luggage office to inquire about my bag. I was told by an agent, again with a great deal of indifference, that I should pay no attention to the displays because the bags didn't necessarily go to those particular ramps! In addition to being somewhat annoyed by that little piece of information, I wasn't especially pleased with the lack of any interest in assistance at all. After looking at other ramps, I filled out my paperwork for my lost bags and quickly made my way out of a bad experience. I understand equipment malfunctions. I understand lost bags. I don't understand indifference.

When I got back from that trip, I told the story to one of my clients, who happens to be a pretty influential businessman in town. He is a personal friend of the local head of the airline with which I had the bad experience. His response was, "I know so-and-so, and he's a good guy."

The issue is not whether or not the senior executive is a "good guy." The issue is the fact that he (or she) is not the company to the customer, or to me in that instance. The company is not the slogan or the founder or the CEO or the logo. The company is the person the customer is dealing with . . . at that moment. The receptionist is the company. The maintenance man is the company. The delivery person is the company. Shouldn't the head of the airline realize that these people, who didn't seem to care a bit about me or my problem, represented his company to me?

I was noticing and experiencing this kind of indifference more and more, and I didn't like it.

ZERO TOLERANCE FOR INDIFFERENCE

Could it be that the companies that don't own their customers focus on zero defects? I was beginning to think so. They tend to focus so much on avoiding problems that they forget, or overlook, the value to their customers in dealing with problems with courtesy and kindness, and elimination of indifference.

I was learning that companies that own their customers focus on zero indifference. They tend to focus so much on eliminating indifference that they find their quest for zero defects to be much easier. Their mission is to serve, not to avoid problems. They realize that service is about eliminating indifference, not problems.

I began wondering how much tolerance companies that focus on zero indifference have for employees who display attitudes of indifference. I was to find the answer to be just the same . . . zero. This appears to be a distinct difference on the part of the companies that "get it" when it comes to service.

HIRING THE RIGHT PEOPLE

One of the traits of the companies who "get it" is their relentless pursuit of employees with good attitudes. As I continued my journey, it became clearer that one of the keys to great service was to have the right employees, employees who reflect the same values that are at the core of the company.

Some companies that I have observed seem to be satisfied with just filling openings and doing tasks. (This is especially predominant in the fast-food industry.) Others, however, emphasize what needs to be done to make the initial hire as effective as possible. They strive toward hiring employees who exhibit the traits of the values the company holds dear and do not tolerate for long the employee without those values, whom they made the mistake of hiring. I found that companies offering values-based customer service move quickly to correct hiring mistakes. They want to reduce the chances of bad character leading to bad characters in their workplace.

A CEO whom I interviewed on my talk show discussed the attitudes of employees. He stated clearly that while he was a compassionate individual, he was virtually intolerant of poor attitudes because of the impact they had on other employees. He would work with those who had slipped in with poor attitudes, but he made it clear that the efforts weren't going to go on long before a change was made if a difference were not noticeable.

I did find, as I asked around, that this is more easily done in small to mid-sized companies than in publicly traded companies. Executives in public companies said that corporate policy made them extremely cautious regarding terminations unless firmly warranted. On the other hand, principals in smaller businesses expressed little concern regarding eliminating bad hiring selections from their "family."

COMMON TRAITS OF TOP SERVICE PROVIDERS

There are lots of companies who "get it" to some degree, although not nearly enough. However, there are obviously too many to cover in one book. That said, while I interviewed many companies for this project, I decided to narrow the ones I would include in this book to those that would be recognized nationally, with one exception.

Other than that, the companies that were brought to my attention are from all over the spectrum: retail, fast food, service; and public, private, nonprofit—you name it. All are companies that get it. Here are some of the common traits I found in all of these companies:

- *They believe in principles, which come from the top, often from the founder.*

- *They believe that these principles must be kept at the top of the mind of each employee in order to be meaningful.*

- *They believe in the dignity of the jobs of their employees; each job is important.*

- *They believe that their corporate entity has a purpose.*

- *They have identified a unique mission for their company that separates them from their competition.*

- *They recognize the importance of empowerment on the part of their employees.*

- *They understand the "law of attraction" and how they attract the type of employees and customers they do.*

- *They believe in the value of kindness.*

Make no mistake about it: These companies are not the norm. They do not represent the current state of customer service in this country; they represent the very finest and what all companies should try to be. They also serve as examples of what all companies *can* be if they are willing to make some changes in their culture. Unfortunately, not enough will.

WHAT SHOULD CUSTOMERS EXPECT?

At this point in my journey I had reached the conclusion that service was at an all-time low and that I certainly didn't do business with any company that "owned me." Each time I speak to groups, I ask the question, "How do you gauge the current state of customer service? Is it better than ever, worse, or holding its own?" The answer is always "worse." On my radio talk show, I often ask, "How's service these days?" The inevitable answer is "Bad."

I often wonder, as I observe this situation, how we have gotten into this mess as a society. Is the United States not *the* service economy of the world? Is it true, as I have heard, that there are more people employed at McDonalds than in the steel industry in the United States? Can this malaise be caused by the difference in upbringing of the newest generation of employees in the United States?

I wanted to blame this on something. I wanted to point the finger at a culture, a phenomenon, a misaligned star, or something that would cause me to accept the fact that something has happened, outside of the control of businesses, to explain the indifference, disrespect, and lack of courtesy that I am getting today in the name of service by most companies. I want better service, feel that I deserve better service, and don't like it when I don't get it from companies that I am paying.

I'm basically a pretty easy customer. I don't expect perfection. I am aware of the human element in service, and I am very forgiving of errors, especially errors of commission. Accidents will happen, and I understand that they do. I don't expect products to be perfect or to operate perfectly. I know that defects occur, and I don't go crazy when things don't work.

What I *can't* stand is the indifference that I get from many service providers when something does go wrong. I want to feel important. Here is what I don't want:

- I don't want an order taken by someone who won't acknowledge my presence.

- I don't want to be ignored.

- I don't want to have trouble getting someone to talk to, either on the phone or in person.

- I don't want to wonder what is being done when I need help.

- I don't want to be left on hold for long periods of time.

- I don't want to have to ask someone whether he or she is listening.

- I don't want to constantly have to ask the other person what he or she said.

I am consistently amazed at how companies that I speak to these days are completely ambivalent about the role that customer service plays, or rather should play, in their business. What's even more surprising to me is how often I find this ambivalence among smaller companies. The reason for my surprise is that the smaller companies are the ones that can most easily create changes in culture. It is these companies that should be able to create the atmospheres of service that can more easily transcend through employees to customers. What tends to occur is a feeling of panic when this smaller company loses a major customer due to indifference in their customer service. It tries to correct the problem, and it is too late.

COMMON PERCEPTIONS OF CUSTOMER SERVICE

I asked a number of friends and acquaintances why they thought service was where it is today. Their comments were intriguing and not surprising:

- *"These kids have no upbringing! They have no respect for anyone else and don't put any value at all in the job they are doing."*

- *"Most of these (public) companies are so interested in the bottom line that they have cut service to the bone. As long as they are making money, they don't care about service."*

- *"You can't find good people anymore."*

- *"People don't care."*

- *"There is no passion for excellence."*

These are just some of the answers I got, but they probably best reflect the perception of customer service today.

SERVICE AT ITS WORST

I rely on a lot of technology in my business these days. I use a wireless phone with e-mail access, a PC, laptop, regular telephone, PDA, and broadband cable access to the Internet. I can't fix any of them when something goes wrong, and I literally dread the days when I have to make service calls to any of the companies that provide them. They *all* have the same problems with their service:

- They are time-consuming when looking for help.

- They are difficult to get in touch with.

- They are difficult to get answers from.

- They don't follow up.

- They don't seem to care about my problem.

My business is dependent upon each of these services, so I am greatly affected when there is a problem with any of these services. I hate to call any of them. They don't own me, they rent me. I would gladly change any of them and pay more for a company that would respond to me quickly, enthusiastically, and accurately. However, it appears that these companies would rather sell to new customers with competitive prices than keep their existing ones by providing exceptional service at a little more cost.

GETTING SOME DIRECTION

I had given up on chronicling a number of "classic" customer service stories. This should have told me something then and there, but I didn't really get it yet. I simply thought I had asked the wrong companies or that my "pitch" wasn't good enough.

Whatever it was, I knew that I wasn't getting what I wanted, and I was getting a little frustrated.

I took a break from the book for a while. This whole "indifference" concept had me intrigued. I knew I was on to something with the elimination-of-indifference theme, but I still didn't want to write just another "how to" book. I wanted examples. I knew that I was getting close to discovering the "secret ingredient" that all the best companies had. I found myself questioning what that secret was, what was in the mix for great customer service.

I had a speaking engagement in Alabama and decided to drive, as I prefer to do rather than fly. (I get more polite service that way.) I stopped at a well-known national fast-food restaurant to get a cup of coffee. I stood behind a gentleman, and we both observed the impatience—and almost anger—that the server displayed behind the counter. When the gentleman was asked whether he wanted anything else with his order, he gave an entertaining and thought-provoking answer: "Yeah," he said. "How about a little kindness with my fries?"

I was struck by what this gentleman said, and I thought I may have found the secret ingredient to great customer service—kindness. I also had a reason to keep on searching for what made the difference in service and decided that I would keep on going. I just didn't realize how close I was.

COMPANIES THAT STAND OUT FROM THE CROWD

I was led to a book entitled *Don't Worry, Make Money* (New York: Hyperion, 1998), in which author Richard Carlson discusses how to leave a *great* impression, not just a good one. He writes:

> When people think of you, you want them to genuinely want to do business, spend time with you, and help you. You want

your customers, clients, coworkers, colleagues, even
competitors, to think and speak highly of you to others. The
way to do this is very simple: Make living your life with
absolute integrity and kindness your first priority. Put others
first, whenever possible. Be genuinely interested in the lives of
other people. Be very present moment oriented with others.
Look them in the eye and really focus on what they're saying.
Care about them as individuals. Ask about their families.
Listen, listen, and listen. Finally, make your actions match
your good intentions. Stand out from the crowd. Be the one
to thank your customers and the people with whom you work.

I paid special attention to the part of that quote that said,
"Stand out from the crowd." That's what I was looking for . . .
the companies that stood out from the crowd. I knew that they
were out there; I just was looking in the wrong places. Once I
began to recognize what I was looking for, they began to show
up more and more.

CHAPTER TWO

A TOP-DOWN COMMITMENT TO SERVICE

"I do not consider a sale complete until goods are worn out and customer still satisfied."
—L.L. BEAN

I STARTED ASKING MY COLLEAGUES, clients, and friends to name the companies that came to mind when I mentioned "good customer service." I wanted to find out which companies had this kind of immediate identification when it came to service. And I wanted to find what created this impression.

I didn't have to wait long for my first answer. It came in the form of a question asked by a friend at a dinner party. I was talking about my frustrations at finding the very best in service providers, the ones that really made a difference in the way they did business. The question my friend asked was this:

"Have you tried L.L.Bean?"

A CHRISTMAS STORY

An associate of mine named David came in after Christmas break a couple of years ago with the following story. David had bought his Dad a sweater from an online store. The sweater arrived the day before Christmas Eve and was the wrong size. His family actually celebrated Christmas and swapped presents on Christmas Eve. David was in a jam.

David decided that he would call the company he had bought the sweater from, knowing that it was too late to get another sweater. He was hoping just to get to talk to someone without holding forever and to place his order to get his Dad's sweater as soon as possible after Christmas.

He called the company . . . L.L.Bean.

"Merry Christmas," answered the customer rep on the first ring. "How can I help you?"

David told the story, asking how to exchange the sweater and how to get a new one sent out after Christmas for his Dad.

"After Christmas?" was the reply. "You simply package the sweater up and send it back when you can. In the meantime, I'll get another one out tonight via FedEx for your Father to have tomorrow."

No questions, no problem. Simply *Let's take care of your problem*—courtesy the L.L.Bean way.

And the L.L.Bean way it is. I've told this story to quite a few of my peers, friends, and associates, and they say, "That's the way they do business. They're known for that kind of service."

BUILT-IN VALUES

I wanted to know more. I wanted to know how this happened . . . how a company could have that kind of reputation with so many customers. So, I began by looking at its website. I didn't need to look any further.

According to the L.L.Bean website:

> Leon Leonwood Bean, or L.L., was born in the small township of Greenwood, Maine, in 1872. The values our founder was raised to believe in were simple and deeply engrained. . . .

Nature was something to be revered. Family ties were a priority. Being neighborly was a matter of course. And 'do unto others' was not just a saying but a way of life. When L.L. launched his company with the first Maine Hunting Shoe in 1912, he believed so strongly in the Golden Rule that he made it the foundation of his business.

Get it? Values. Values that can be posted for the world to see. The golden rule that L.L. Bean instilled as the basis of his business philosophy is simply this: "*Sell good merchandise at a reasonable profit, treat your customers like human beings, and they will always come back for more.*"

This is called owning your customer.

GUARANTEED 100 PERCENT SATISFACTION

L.L.Bean answers up to 180,000 customer calls every day . . . on the first or second ring. The company's guarantee on a product begins when that call is answered . . . and lasts for the lifetime of the product.

The stories of L.L.Bean's customer service are legendary, from the shirt owner who utilized his guarantee thirty years after the purchase of the shirt, claiming "his" lifetime guarantee (the company gladly exchanged the shirt) to the numerous callers who call the service department just to talk to the friendly folks. But sometimes these kinds of urban legends can be deceiving. Much can be promised that is never delivered. I had heard enough of these stories that I decided to try calling to see for myself.

I decided to give it a try. The next day, I looked up L.L.Bean on the Internet and gave the customer service number a call. On the first ring, I got June. I was actually a little unprepared, so I just hung up. It was 9:00 p.m., and I thought it was too easy to get through, being so late. I couldn't resist one more try, so I made another call just to check. On the first ring, I got Ashley, then I apologized and hung up.

I decided that I would call again during daytime hours the next day to see what things would be like then. Prior to that, however, I took a closer look at the guarantee of the company's products on its website and found a plaque that L.L. Bean had hung in a store in 1916. It read, "I do not consider a sale complete until goods are worn out and customer still satisfied."

I have to tell you that I couldn't wait for the next day, so I called one more time. Same results as before; on the first ring, my call was answered. That time, I got Valerie.

"Miss, could you settle something for me please?" I asked. "If I purchase something from you, wear it for a while, and then decide I don't like it, will you take it back?"

"Certainly" she replied. "We want you to be happy with everything you buy at L.L.Bean."

No mention of receipt, time deadline, proof of purchase, original packing, nothing. Simply, "We want you to be happy."

Go to the L.L.Bean website at www.llbean.com. You'll read: "L.L.'s values live on, and at L.L.Bean today, we still measure success by the satisfaction of our customers."

As L.L.'s grandson Leon Gorman, chairman of the board of L.L.Bean, says, "Serving customers is a day-in, day-out, ongoing, never-ending, unremitting, persevering, compassionate kind of activity."

Take a look at that last sentence, and you will begin to see what separates this provider of world-class customer service from so many other companies. Look at the commitment that is made in this one sentence: "ongoing," "never-ending," and "compassionate." These are simple, but powerful, words when it comes to service.

MAKING CUSTOMERS HAPPY

As I experienced L.L.Bean, I noticed that everything about the contacts I had with that company reflected comfort and making customers happy. Everything. From the website to the stores, every customer touch reflects customer comfort and satisfaction. It is as if every step in the customer process had been reviewed.

L.L.Bean has indeed taken every step of the customer process, tested it, and created a process that is consistent with what it wants to provide. The process of selling clothes and items has been converted into a total customer service experience.

I have to admit that I was more than a little impressed with L.L.Bean. I also have to admit that I couldn't resist the urge to keep calling its customer service department over and over. Could it answer my calls with such courtesy each time?

I called the customer service line during the middle of the next day. Priscilla answered the call on the first ring. I asked to speak to a supervisor, and she politely said okay. I got Karen, who was just as gracious. I told her I was researching information for my book, and she said she would do whatever she could to help me.

We had a brief conversation during which she told me, among other things, that one problem that the call center had was that it had so many people who will call just to talk because the people are so nice!

I also discovered that the service reps at L.L.Bean are empowered to make decisions regarding service. They use their own judgment in areas such as refunds and returns without worrying about being corrected.

I spoke to the community relations manager for L.L.Bean. She shared with me the story of L.L. Bean starting his company by designing a special boot for hunting. He sent out a flyer that promised satisfaction with his new boot. He got off to a pretty good start for a new business and sold 100 pairs of boots with his satisfaction guarantee. He got requests for money back from 90 of those customers. It seems that the design that Bean was so sure of had some flaws—the boots fell apart quickly. Bean was left with a choice: Give up or go forward.

Although it almost put him out of business, Bean kept going. He had made a promise, and he was going to stand behind it. He borrowed money, corrected the problem, sold more boots, and kept his satisfaction guarantee. It was because of this guarantee that his business grew and prospered. Bean never lost sight of his commitment to quality, and that foundation forms the principles that the L.L.Bean company values today.

WHAT CAN WE LEARN?

The principles that L.L. Bean practiced when he founded this company are still alive today. Subsequent leaders of the company have carried them forward. During my quest to find the top service providers, I found a lot of companies with values in place today that are a continuation of the value system of the founders of the company. And I found there is a top-down commitment in the companies that provide value-based service.

As I was writing this chapter, I was interviewed to be a speaker at an international convention on customer service later in the year. I found myself in a philosophical discussion about customer service with the program director of the convention. She asked whether I would be comfortable discussing my theory that values come from the core with an audience of several hundred CEOs of major businesses. I suggested to her that I would not be uncomfortable, but that some of them might.

Look around at the companies that don't get it, and you'll probably find the feeling that it must be "someone else's fault" other than that of the person or persons at the top. I sense this discomfort often as I am asked to speak to companies about providing exceptional customer service. I detect that what management wants to hear is less about how its values affect the company and more about the "step-by-step" process that employees can take to provide that service. Managers want action for their staff, not challenges for them. This leads to a lot of surprise when it is found that service has to start at the top. It cannot start in the middle.

I recently had a conversation with Kathy Lewis, who is the CEO of Capstone Mortgage Institute in Atlanta. In addition to being a dynamic business leader, Kathy operates her business based on a clear core of values that she would be pleased to discuss with you at any time. When asked how she treats customers who have completed her training course and are unhappy, she simply said, "We'll retrain them until they are happy or give them their money back." This commitment is very straightforward and simple.

But unlike other business leaders who are afraid that they're going to "get screwed" (their words) if they make satisfaction guarantees, Kathy operates on the premise that if you give, you get! If you give guarantees to your customers, you get trust and loyalty in return.

In his book *Customers for Life* (Pocket Books: New York, 1991), author Carl Sewell advises readers to borrow ideas on customer service but to make sure that you pick from the best. This is what I did as I gathered great examples of customer service at its finest. Each of the companies that I chronicle offers the rest of us a challenge that we can choose to accept in our companies.

The L.L.Bean Standard: The standard that L.L.Bean sets is to offer an unconditional guarantee on its work. If, for any reason, you are not satisfied, return the product. Period. Let's take a closer look at what this means for a company. Unconditional means just that . . . no conditions. If, for any reason, you're not happy, you don't pay. If you don't like the product, bring it back. If you're not happy with the meal, it's on us.

Most companies are afraid of this because they think their customers will take advantage of them, and that they'll lose money.

The L.L.Bean Challenge: If you believe in your product and service, the answer is easy. Promise your customers that they'll be happy with what you provide or that they'll get their money back. Of course, you are going to have some unscrupulous individuals or companies who will abuse the policy. L.L.Bean does. Build them into your costs.

There is a story about a certain celebrity who gets her clothes from one of the finest stores around, a store that has a liberal return policy for its customers. The standing joke is that this starlet can be seen on TV Saturday night wearing a dress that she bought on Thursday and that she will return on Monday. Unfortunately, there are some who will abuse any guarantee that is offered.

But you'll find that standing behind your service is going to make a statement about your firm. You believe in what you do and are willing to do more than to say to your customers, "You'll be pleased." You'll tell customers that their satisfaction is 100 percent guaranteed.

CHAPTER THREE

EMPLOYEES ON
A MISSION

"*Help me find my place in life, and I will build you
a shrine where the poor and the helpless and the
hopeless may come for comfort and aid.*"
—DANNY THOMAS

I "GOT IT" during the first minute of my tour of the hospital.

The hospital I am referring to is St. Jude Children's Research Center located in Memphis, Tennessee. While a well-known institution in its own right, St. Jude is probably not usually associated with customer service. However, I found that there is much we can learn from St. Jude about instilling a strong sense of mission in every employee, no matter what his or her position in the organization is.

A SHINING BEACON

Located in downtown Memphis, the hospital provides treatment and research involving children's diseases. St. Jude is considered quite a jewel by Memphians, and you don't have to go far to meet a volunteer who is passionate about the work being done there. Drive around Memphis, and you will see signs of St. Jude all around, from bumper stickers to license plates.

For readers outside of Memphis, St. Jude is probably best recognized for its telethons that are held throughout the year on national television, or perhaps for other charitable events such as bike races and marathons. It is one of the most recognizable charitable operations in the world.

I have spoken a number of times to groups at St. Jude and have always been impressed by their obvious dedication to their work. These are people who realize the importance of what they do, every day. You can literally sense that feeling when you walk in the door of the hospital. From the medical staff to clerical personnel to information technology support, all through the organization, they know what they do. They save children's lives.

IT STARTED WITH ONE MAN'S PRAYER

The work that goes on at St. Jude can only be described as the culmination of kindness and the result of a prayer made by a struggling entertainer during the last years of the Great Depression.

This young man, Danny Thomas, had dreamed of being an entertainer since his very early days. But those were not easy times, and the future didn't look much better for this talented, but seemingly hopeless, dreamer. His job prospects were poor, and his wife was expecting their first child. He didn't have the money to pay for her hospital stay.

His struggles led him to a church in Detroit, where he prayed this prayer to St. Jude Thaddeus, the patron saint of hopeless cases: "Help me find my place in life, and I will build you a shrine where the poor and the helpless and the hopeless may come for comfort and aid." Please note that he didn't say, "I'll give you some of the money I make," or "I'll make a donation to a shrine." He didn't ask for wealth or fame or fortune . . . simply to "find my place."

For those who are not familiar with Danny Thomas, it can safely be said that he "found his place." As an entertainer, Thomas was the star of a weekly television show that ran for eleven years. At his peak, he was one of the most highly recognized figures in entertainment. But even during his rise to success, he never forgot his promise . . . he never let it die.

Thomas did more than just sell his name for St. Jude. He was *the* driving force behind the building of this hospital. He didn't just give some money with instructions to build a hospital. He had made a promise . . . a promise to build a shrine.

And so a shrine he built. St. Jude Children's Research Center was the first institution built for the single purpose of conducting research for childhood diseases, mainly cancer. Constructed in its original design in 1962, it has treated over 20,000 children from all over the world. Built at a time when childhood cancer was considered a hopeless cause (there's that prayer, ". . . where the hopeless can come"), survivor rates are currently over 75 percent. Compare that figure to a death rate of 95 percent when the hospital opened its doors.

Readers who are unfamiliar with St. Jude will be interested to know that not one of the children's families has ever paid a dime for treatment at the hospital ("poor . . . helpless . . . hopeless" . . . there's that prayer again).

One more thing: It is estimated that for every child saved at St. Jude there are 1,000 saved around the world. Simply stated, it is estimated that the research done there not only saves lives but also avoids the same illness in others. This is the living impact that one man's prayer of over forty years ago has today.

EXPERIENCING ST. JUDE FIRSTHAND

I had never associated customer service with St. Jude. I had always thought of a "customer" as someone who paid for a service and thus had an expectation of what he or she would receive for that payment.

My interest in St. Jude, regarding this book, came as a result of the number of people who had mentioned it when I requested examples of superior customer service. "I don't know if you can call the patients 'customers,' but I *do* know that something special is going on out there" would be the typical response.

So, even if St. Jude doesn't have any customers per se, the name kept coming up as I asked where special service was being performed. I wanted to see for myself.

A week prior to my tour, I had addressed a group of employees at the American Lebanese Syrian Associated Charities (ALSAC), which is the fund-raising organization for St. Jude. I was invited to a private tour of the hospital by Marilyn Elledge, who is the VP of Donor Services for ALSAC and had heard me speak at an earlier event.

Marilyn knows her way around the hospital as a result of her fifteen years of employment there. Her enthusiasm for showing me around was apparent as we met in the lobby of a building adjacent to the hospital itself. During the first minutes of my tour through the hospital, it became apparent that Marilyn Elledge (as well as other employees who have patient contact) makes a point to get to know the patients and their families. Many familiar and very personal exchanges and greetings took place as we toured.

At one point, a lovely young woman, dressed sharply in a business suit and wearing an employee name tag, stopped and said hello to Marilyn. The two obviously were pleased to see each other and spoke quietly as I stood by. Marilyn introduced me to the woman, Lindsey Wilkerson. Lindsey shook my hand, mentioned that she was an employee at St. Jude/ALSAC, and proudly said, "I am a product of the work that goes on here."

Lindsey Wilkerson was one of those patients whom Marilyn got to know over the years. Lindsey was diagnosed with cancer as a ten-year-old and admitted to the hospital in 1991. Like many other patients, she has been part of the family ever since. As is often the case, Marilyn befriended Lindsey during her sickness. Lindsey recovered and took a job in the Event Liaison Department. The friendship flourished.

With no small amount of pride, Marilyn showed me a picture of herself taken recently at Lindsey's wedding . . . wearing the bridesmaid's gown that she wore as part of the wedding party. They were both also eager to point out that Lindsey was enthusiastically given away on that special day by Richard Shadyak, the president of ALSAC. The president made time to give away one of his family.

For someone as lovely and vital as Lindsey to have survived a disease that was once considered incurable was a miracle. It became more miraculous when I learned during the tour that St. Jude didn't have a rehabilitation center when the hospital first opened because one wasn't needed. This changed after the success that St. Jude experienced during the early 1970s, and the rehab department opened during that time. It now serves about 750 patients per month.

SERVING ST. JUDE'S CUSTOMERS

To raise the millions of dollars required to provide treatment and research, thousands of volunteers and donors must be contacted and supported, therefore effectively resulting in St. Jude and ALSAC having two groups of customers to serve . . . patients and donors.

Serve them St. Jude does. It requires over 400 donor services representatives, both employees and volunteers, to coordinate the efforts that support the children being helped at the hospital. Add to this group the hundreds of professional and staff employees involved in treatment and research, as well as the innumerable volunteers around the world who contribute time and energy to raise money for these kids, and you have a web of support that spans the globe. Literally hundreds of thousands of volunteers from all backgrounds support over 25,000 fund-raising events annually. And when you meet any of the representatives of these groups, you will sense the pride and kindness with which they do their work. The values put in place through the prayer of one young man many years ago are still alive and well in this shrine.

There is a quiet dignity about St. Jude. You don't hear political grumbling, employee complaints, or threats from the management there. Everybody connected with St. Jude quietly goes about their business in a way that makes Memphians glad to be the home of this hospital and research center. From local businesses to the professional golf tour, everywhere around town, the pride that Memphians have in this life-affecting institution is reflected.

Walk through the patient wings of the hospital and notice the murals on the walls, painted with the main themes at a height that young children can enjoy. Notice the sign at the doors of the medicine room that reads, "Please park all trikes before entering." Pay attention to the smiles on the faces of employees and patients, smiles that come through great pain and inconvenience, and sometimes fear of death. Note the bulletin boards, where staff can post pictures of patients. Observe the looks of love and gratitude on the faces of virtually all the parents with whom you come into contact.

The employees at St. Jude act as if they are on a mission. They are certainly polite and will stop and speak to you, but you can clearly sense that they know what it is they are all about . . . every one of them. It also should be pointed out that these employees are not motivated by stock options, dividends, or money.

St. Jude is considered a great place to work, but not because of higher-than normal pay rates. There's another reason folks want to work there.

I asked an employee in information technology what it is like to have a job at St. Jude. She does not have direct contact with the children and the hospital, but rather provides support for the operation. But her response is typical: "Oh, my gosh! I can't tell you what it means to me, especially on a bad day, to walk over into the dining room and have lunch with those patients and their families. If I ever feel a need to know my place, that is all I have to do."

WHAT CAN WE LEARN?

As I drove away following my tour, I felt really good about what I had seen and experienced at this wonderful institution. But I also knew that there were lessons to be learned by businesses of all types in observing how business is done at St. Jude:

- *I saw firsthand the power of every employee being made to feel like family.* I saw the importance of *that* family embracing their customers, in this case patients, as extended family.

- *I observed the benefit of a clear and strong mission.* Everyone in this organization understands his or her role in serving these kids. Physician to staff, executive to volunteer, everyone understands what they do and how it serves what they are all about, which is saving the lives of children.

I asked myself whether employees at other companies could view their work as "important" as the work being done at St. Jude. I wondered whether the passion there was the result of the fact that they were indeed saving lives. Could employees at a lumber company, retail store, restaurant, or *anywhere* feel that their work was this important? Is it critical that workers think they are saving lives, or is it enough to feel that they are *affecting* lives?

I then reflected on the words of Dr. Wayne Dyer, who writes, "When you change the way you look at things, the things you look at will change." (*The Power of Intention,* Carlsbad, Calif.: Hay House, 2004.) If we can change the way we look at a particular job, the way we see that job will change. Companies providing compassionate customer service get this.

> *A man walked by a construction site and stopped to talk to a worker. "What are you doing?" he asked.*
>
> *"I'm cutting stone" was the worker's reply.*
>
> *To the next worker, he asked the same question. "I'm building a cornerstone" was the response.*
>
> *To the third, he asked the same question. After a brief pause, the worker answered, "I'm building a cathedral."*

APPLYING THESE LESSONS TO BUSINESS

So, how does the St. Jude experience apply to business and customer service? That's easy . . . it begins with making sure that every employee understands the importance of his or her job in providing service. It appears that most employees today are hired with clear instructions on *what* to do on the job daily, but not much emphasis on *why* that job is important or even needed! These folks at St. Jude/ALSAC understand the significance that every job plays in saving kids' lives. Not all jobs in service are life-saving, but they *are* all life-affecting.

How can you accomplish this at your own company? Here are three things you can do:

1. *Make sure your corporate mission is clear to every employee.* What is it that your company does? I'm not referring here to the company mission statement that hangs on the wall of your lobby and that no one can quote, but rather what it is that you are trying to be the "best" at every day that you report to work. (Hint: If you don't have this mission clearly in your head, you are already in trouble.) Do you want to be the fastest, most reliable, cheapest, or friendliest in your industry? Identify what it is that your company can do that will make it stand out from the others. This is crucial for long-term success, and it is what is sorely lacking in most companies.

    One of the best examples ever of this mission identification is the story of Avis. While Avis was founded in the 1940s, it came into prominence in the early 1960s as a result of advertising that admitted that it was *not* the largest rental car company in the world (Hertz held that honor), but that because of that it had to try harder to serve its customers. That phrase "We try harder" is still Avis's identifying mission statement and the objective of each employee in the company. Try harder than the competition, and everything else will take of itself.

2. *Identify how every job in your company supports your mission.* Go through your organizational chart and look at every single job. If it doesn't contribute to the mission, either change it or eliminate it. If you are completing this exercise for the first time, begin to imagine the impact on your company if every job focused on the mission . . . if every person tried harder and were friendlier, whatever the mission.

    For years, the focus of McDonald's was on being

the cleanest fast-food restaurant around. How many times have you walked into a McDonald's and seen people cleaning up? More important, how many times have you been driving with your family and heard, "Mommy, I need to go to the bathroom" and decided to stop at McDonald's to take a break and get something to eat? The food might not have been the best, but the restrooms were the cleanest.

3. *Communicate the importance of each job to the person who does that job.* Make sure that every individual employee knows the importance of his or her job in successfully completing your mission. Do we have too many cathedral builders who think they are just cutting stone? Do we as managers stress the importance of our employees' jobs from a standpoint of what they mean to the big picture as distinguished from what they mean to our bottom line?

The St. Jude Standard: St. Jude sets a remarkable standard as an example of an organization that realizes its mission. Every employee at St. Jude goes to work understanding his or her role. Whether they be administration, information technology support, maintenance workers, or medical professionals, whatever they do, they know their purpose. It is to save children's lives.

The St. Jude Challenge: Do your employees know why they come to work every day? Are their missions to just do a task or to make a difference to someone somehow? Is your company in business to achieve something or simply do something? Imagine the difference it could make if each employee in a company understood a greater value for why he or she came to work.

I'm not referring here to some grandiose posturing that we are in business to "save the world" or a mission nearly as noble as saving children's lives. I am referring to an understanding that each job is important to the mission of the company, which *should* be to serve a purpose. That purpose may be as simple as a mission to make the best pies in the world; let each employee understand how he or she contributes to that. The purpose may be to insure families, prepare and deliver food, or install software. Whatever the experience might be, each employee must understand how he or she as an individual is a key part of making that experience better. This is the challenge. I have never seen it done better than at St. Jude.

CHAPTER FOUR

NEVER ON SUNDAY

"*Our operators consider themselves to be mentors to the next generation.***"**

—TRUETT CATHY

ONE OF THE THINGS I LEARNED quickly in my quest for top service providers is that the fast-food business is not the most respected industry as far as customer service goes.

I don't eat a lot of fast food on a regular basis. When I travel by car, however, I tend to stop at McDonald's because their restrooms tend to be clean. While I'm there, I'll get a cup of coffee or sometimes a sandwich. I'm used to what they deliver. I'm not going to knock McDonald's. I'm sure there are very many wonderful people who both work for, as well as own, McDonald's franchises. Unfortunately, I tend to get the guy or gal who is having a bad day or wishes I weren't there. I also tend to get the one who doesn't very effectively speak the language that I use.

FAST FOOD WITH A DIFFERENCE

I did begin to hear a lot about another fast-food chain as I searched for the best in service. My fiancée, Debra, was regularly picking up trays of chicken nuggets from Chick-fil-A. She kept suggesting that I look into this chain since it was different. I didn't know what she meant by "different," but I thought I would take a look.

I can't explain why I hadn't been to a Chick-fil-A before I began this book, but I know now what I have missed. If you have been to a Chick-fil-A, you know what I am talking about. If you haven't, go there and you'll see for yourself. Let me tell you in advance that it's a lot more than the food.

When you go to a Chick-fil-A, you are going to find a clear difference between the people who work there and those at virtually any other fast-food restaurant. I wanted to find out what caused this difference, and I did.

Chick-fil-A is a privately held, Georgia-based company. It is not quite a household name, but there are over 1,000 stores across the country. Basically, all they sell is a chicken sandwich, but they do it to the tune of over a billion dollars a year in revenue. Once I began to ask around about customer service, however, this company kept coming up more than any other, more than the household names such as McDonald's, KFC, and Burger King.

Significantly, the two most common comments that were repeated to me about Chick-fil-A were "They really take care of their customers" and "You realize that they close every Sunday, don't you?" I wanted to find out more, and then I learned the Truett Cathy story.

HOW MUCH ARE YOUR VALUES WORTH TO YOU?

Truett Cathy had been in the restaurant business for 21 years when he opened his first Chick-fil-A restaurant in Atlanta's Greenbrier Mall in 1967. When Cathy founded Chick-fil-A, he did so with values based both on faith and on the importance of work in relation to life. Growing up in the south in the 1930s was tough for the Cathy family, but young Truett learned values that stayed with him throughout his life. One of these was the importance of his worship time on Sunday. The other, learned during his early years as the co-owner of a small restaurant, was the importance of respect for employees.

Even as he struggled to keep the doors of his first restaurant open, Cathy remained dedicated to taking Sunday off for himself and his employees. He remains loyal to this policy even today, with all Chick-fil-A locations closed on potentially the busiest day of their week. His position on this is the first of many subtle tips I learned about the law of attraction and how it works in business.

Cathy says, "We find closing on Sunday attracts those people who give attention to spiritual growth and are family-oriented. Admittedly, closing all of our restaurants every Sunday makes us a rarity in this day and age. But it's a little habit that has always served us well, so we're planning to stick with it."

Cathy operates his business under what he calls "four tenets." These are:

1. Instead of selling franchises, Chick-fil-A will form joint ventures with independent operators.

2. Stores will only be opened in major shopping malls. [This has been modified.]

3. Growth will be financed primarily internally.

4. The chief emphasis will be on people.

It should be noted that none of them refers to profits.

In defending his decision to remain a private company as

opposed to going public, Cathy made the following statement in 2002:

> In the early days, we did not offer stock for sale because I could not predict how fast the company might grow or what dividends we might pay to anyone who might invest. . . . If I had a widow invest her savings in Chick-fil-A, and the company didn't pay the return she expected, I would feel obligated to make up the difference to her. Even if we paid less than she could earn in a savings certificate, I would feel compelled to bail her out. Feeling that way, I might as well sign the bank note and be personally responsible rather than take other people's money.

(From *Eat Mor Chikin: Inspire More People* (Decatur, Ga.: Looking Glass Books, 2002.)

FOCUS ON EMPLOYEES

One of the first things I learned about Chick-fil-A is the concern that the operators have for their employees. This comes directly from the top (pay close attention to this . . . this is neither the first nor last time it will come up in this book) of the organization. They realize that the majority of their employees are young and not going to be lifetime employees. What they attempt to do, then, is to make the employment experience at Chick-fil-A meaningful for the workers' future employers. *Yes, you read that correctly*.

While most fast-food companies feel that the way to help the store is to focus on training aimed at the store and its improvement, Chick-fil-A feels that the way to help the store is to help the employee first. For example, I learned that there is a focus on training employees in such disciplines as money management. The focus, then, is the employee, not the store. Helping one, the employee, improves both.

The fast-food industry is notorious for having to recruit high-school and lower-paid employees in order to stay competitive. As a result, these companies suffer from high turnover and poorly trained employees. Chick-fil-A, however, has chosen to mentor the people it hires, and as a result it has offered scholarships to over 16,000 employees. This focus on employees is part of what sets the company apart.

I interviewed a Chick-fil-A operator during the course of writing this book. I learned a lot about the values that make Chick-fil-A and its employees different from other fast-food companies. The operator I interviewed had previously worked for another fast-food operation, a household name. He told me that in the ten years that he worked there, he had met the president of the corporation twice. During his first year as an operator at Chick-fil-A, the president of the company, Dan Cathy, called him on Christmas Day to wish him and his family a Merry Christmas. "How do you think that made me feel?" he asked me.

I also learned that Chick-fil-A operators are not allowed to own more than one or two stores (one is the norm). Unlike most competitors, operators don't own territories, they own stores. The result is a presence in the store of the operator, where his or her principles and values can be observed by employees. Chick-fil-A carefully screens potential operators regarding their representation of the values of the company. You can imagine the impact on young employees who observe values of dignity, respect, courtesy, and kindness at work exhibited every day in the stores by the operators themselves. You won't see a hands-off boss giving orders to a staff of people. You'll see an eager operator picking up trays, speaking to customers and employees alike, and setting an example for the staff to follow.

BUILDING CUSTOMER LOYALTY

Chick-fil-A is an example of an excellent company with an "okay" product. Its stores sell chicken sandwiches . . . where can you *not* get a chicken sandwich? Yet, they attract a customer type that keeps coming back to them.

I mentioned that one of the interesting aspects of Chick-fil-A is its restriction on the number of stores that franchisees may own. They are required to spend time in the store and with their customers! Walk into a Chick-fil-A, and you will probably bump into the owner of the restaurant. Have you *ever* gone into one of the big-name fast-food restaurants and met the owner of the franchise? You probably haven't, since they tend to own lots of them and let others run the stores.

I was also made aware of a franchise owners' meeting recently at which *nothing* was discussed other than customer service. *Nothing.* The owners were instructed to come up with anything they could think of to improve customer service, regardless of how small it might seem. They then were instructed to agree on the "best" of those suggestions and implement them in their stores.

I learned that Chick-fil-A began a tradition of offering the first 100 customers who showed up at the grand opening of a new store a free combo meal each week for a year. I watched as a new store opened in Memphis, and literally dozens of people camped out overnight to claim this prize. I further learned that this happens in every city where Chick-fil-A opens and that one of the campers is usually Dan Cathy, Truett's son and the company president. "I might as well be out there with them," he says.

VALUES VS. RELIGION

I think that this might be the time to separate values from religion. I am going to share my personal beliefs very briefly here so that there will be no confusion among readers. I am a Christian but also respect the beliefs of others. I feel no more comfortable with my wallet in a business deal after someone has prayed before we eat than when we don't. I have seen crooks wearing every religious sign you can imagine. While I believe that religion can result in a shift in values, I also believe that values can be learned without religion, and often are.

This is important to understand as one observes the Chick-fil-A model. While practicing Christian beliefs in their personal lives, the principals of Chick-fil-A are not attempting to proselytize through their business, nor do they "preach" as they work. Rather, they put values at the forefront of their business activity for anyone to see and to make their personal decisions on their own. Emphasis is on value and spirit rather than on religion. Dignity rather than doctrine. It may be true that the spiritually void sometimes have a difficult time with the Chick-fil-A culture, but it may be just as true that the culture is responsible for the difference between Chick-fil-A and other fast-food chains.

WILL YOUR COMPANY LEGACY LIVE ON?

Truett Cathy remains as chairman and CEO of Chick-fil-A, but his son Dan has taken over the day-to-day operation of the company. While sustaining rapid growth, the company values remain the same. Pay attention to cleanliness, be cheerful (listen for how many times you hear "My pleasure" when you dine there), and maintain spiritual values. ("We think our food tastes better on Mondays because we are closed on Sundays," Dan Cathy likes to say.)

I agree with those who say that excellence in business is quickly detectable, that it is clear when you walk into a company's office or headquarters. Excellence is reflected by the pride taken in the appearance of the office or waiting area, the realization that this is the first impression that many will have of my company.

When I went to Chick-fil-A headquarters in Atlanta for the first time, I got that immediate recognition of excellence. From the cleanliness of the lobby, to the friendliness of the reception-ist, and on past the lobby to the collection of classic cars on display, the only word to describe my impression was "values." Tradition was displayed in the "museum" off the main lobby where the history of the founding and the growth of the com-pany is tracked via press clippings and photos.

I asked myself, as I looked around the Chick-fil-A home of-fice, how many companies had tradition and values at the core of their operation? How many upheld beliefs and principles that were as clear as those at Chick-fil-A, that their employees simply knew would drive the decisions from the top? My mind wan-dered to the numerous times I had stood in waiting areas of companies and had detected nothing in the form of pride, val-ues, or tradition. No feeling of excellence, nothing detectable. The differences at Chick-fil-A were clear and observable.

ARE YOU WILLING TO CHANGE THE STANDARD?

Sometimes after a dinner out, Debra and I will stop by a fast-food restaurant located near my house. She likes to get a little something sweet to eat, and this spot has some cobbler that she enjoys.

We are often amazed at the poor service we get there. Most of the time, our amazement is at the mistakes made in filling the simple order we place. However, our amazement hit a new high on a recent visit.

First of all, I could not understand a word the drive-up greeter said. I literally had to ask him twice to repeat what he said as we were greeted. Second, we listened with our mouths open when the car behind us was placing its order after we had pulled to the next window, and we actually heard the employees who were preparing the food making derogatory comments about the orders that were placed in the car behind us! This is a regional operation that I'm sure has absolutely no idea what its employees are doing to ruin its image.

The worst part of this story is the fact that it is not surprising to most people. When I tell it, they tend to shake their head and just go, "That's the way it is these days."

That's not "the way it is" at Chick-fil-A. I have been watching Chick-fil-A since I was introduced to the company on this quest for the best in customer service. As I drive past the store near my home every Sunday, I see the lights out and note that the employees are off. All because of values instilled by the company's founder from the very beginning.

═══════════

The Chick-fil-A Standard: Chick-fil-A sets an extremely high bar when it comes to the standard of core values at the expense of profit. Practicing what they believe has cost the principals of this company literally hundreds of millions of dollars; Sunday is traditionally the busiest day of the week for fast-food companies, and the decision to close on Sundays has cost the company dearly.

The Chick-fil-A Challenge: What values does your company live by? What does it practice to the extent that it would sacrifice business, revenue, or a deal to stand behind? Does it "bend" when the time comes to practice what it preaches? Does it "talk" and not "walk"? The challenge here is simple: Assess your corporate value, and measure what you give up to make it happen. What is the price that your company is putting on its value?

Your company probably won't institute something as dramatic as Chick-fil-A's closed-on-Sunday policy. But the idea of focusing on employee growth regardless of how it relates to the company itself is not so far-fetched. Nor is the concept of having franchise owners be part of the scene and not out of the picture. What about the idea of a customer-service event like Chick-fil-A's giving the first 100 customers at any new franchise a free meal once a week for a year?

The concept is simple. The values at the top of an organization must be visible and in action within the organization. Words mean nothing; actions are the measuring stick of values.

From preparing young employees for future employment to closing on Sundays, the values established by Truett Cathy permeate the company he founded. The executives, store owners, managers, and employees live by them every day—including Sunday. They all benefit from these values, as do Chick-fil-A's customers.

CHAPTER FIVE

TALKING ABOUT SERVICE . . . EVERY DAY

"*We are Ladies and Gentlemen serving Ladies and Gentlemen*"

—MOTTO OF THE RITZ-CARLTON

MY FIRST STAY at a Ritz-Carlton was last year for a speaking engagement. I stayed at the Reynolds Plantation Ritz-Carlton outside of Atlanta. I had heard of the mystique of The Ritz-Carlton customer service, but this was the first time I was to experience it firsthand.

I knew that the name "The Ritz-Carlton" had an elegant ring to it, but what could it do that was different from any other hotel? After all, they all do the same things: take a reservation, check you in, provide a room and a restaurant, clean up during the day, check you out. I didn't know what could be so different about The Ritz-Carlton, but I was going to find out for myself.

I was not disappointed in what I experienced.

LEGENDARY CUSTOMER SERVICE

Satisfied customers will always spread the word. As I searched for the top customer service providers, the norm was to have the very best pointed out to me by those who had experienced the service firsthand.

I first heard of the Ritz-Carlton customer service experience from one of my show sponsors. He spoke highly of the hotel's methods for taking extreme care of its customers and gave me a card with The Ritz-Carlton's "practices" on it. It was a small, laminated card with different sections . . . all involving ways to take care of customers. He told me, "You can't believe how they feel about customer service. I know how passionate you are about it, and you need to check them out."

"We are Ladies and Gentlemen serving Ladies and Gentlemen." This is the motto of The Ritz-Carlton. Have a conversation with anyone who works there, and you will hear this phrase. It has a certain meaning that combines elegance with a challenge for Ritz-Carlton employees. Their challenge is to remember constantly to lift themselves up to the level at which they have placed their customers! We serve Ladies and Gentlemen; let us act like Ladies and Gentlemen. Visit any of the Ritz-Carlton locations around the world, and you will sense this treatment. You might not get perfection, but you *will* get respect.

Every day at The Ritz-Carlton begins with the "lineup." This process is the beginning of the shift for every employee in the organization, from the CEO on down. The concept is very simple: About ten minutes at the beginning of the day is spent discussing what is going to happen that day as well as discussing one of the basics of the Ritz-Carlton model of service. These basics are found on the card described above that each employee considers to be part of his or her uniform and that deals with everything from greeting guests to using their names.

This is why when you ask any employee within the Ritz-Carlton organization how often they talk about customer service, the answer is going to be the same: "Every day."

FINDING OUT FOR MYSELF

My amazing experience with Ritz-Carlton customer service began as I was driving to Atlanta for some meetings prior to my speech. I got a message on my voice mail from the concierge welcoming me to The Ritz-Carlton and inviting me to let him know if I needed anything such as reservations or tee-times. I have traveled all over the country, and have *never* had a hotel call me ahead of my arrival to welcome me. I was even more impressed by the fact that I was not part of any group or event, just a single guest staying one night at the hotel. (The event at which I was speaking was not at The Ritz-Carlton itself.)

I had heard about the lineup being the cornerstone of Ritz-Carlton service. In order to see whether what I had heard was true, I decided that I would ask each Ritz-Carlton employee I came into contact with a simple question: "How often do you talk about customer service?" Remember that the employees didn't know I was any kind of customer service advocate, speaker, or author. To them, I was simply a guest. A curious guest, but a guest just the same.

I started with the valet when we checked the car. I next asked the bellman as he greeted us and took our bags. I then asked the concierge and desk clerk. The question was the same, and the answer was the same. Each time, I got the same answer. "Every day."

WHAT KIND OF EXAMPLE DO YOU SET?

The key to the Ritz-Carlton lineup, in addition to its simplicity and effectiveness, is the fact that it begins at the very top of the organization. Every employee who participates knows that the most senior officials of the company have made time that day to go through the exact same process. This is where too many companies that want to initiate service changes go wrong.

I am going to tell you right now that if your organization is not talking about customer service every day, constantly, then you are at risk of being surpassed by another company in your industry. Value-based service is a culture. It is not talk; it is an ongoing belief that what you do is not as important as how you do it. No better example exists than The Ritz-Carlton. "We are Ladies and Gentlemen serving Ladies and Gentlemen." There are hundreds of hotel brands; there is only one Ritz-Carlton.

Recently, I was asked to speak to a group about its customer service process to see whether it could be improved. This was a group of about fifty managers from one corporation who dealt with the same customers every day. Their senior executive had heard me speak at a dinner meeting and wanted me to come in after-hours one evening and to work for a few hours with his staff of managers. Prior to the event itself, I spent time both on the phone and face to face with the senior executive covering the objectives of the session and their importance.

Immediately before his introduction, the senior executive whispered to me, "I just wanted to let you know I'll have to be leaving early tonight. I've been here all day, and I'm going to get some rest."

I was amazed at the sheer ignorance of what I was hearing! How this executive expected his subordinates to "buy in" to the program we were initiating was beyond me. The result was an entertaining and informative evening with an impact that probably took about three days to die. What this unsuspecting (and not-too-smart) executive did was to tell his employees nonverbally, "This isn't important to me. If it were, I'd be here with you."

THE GOLD STANDARDS

Do your employees carry customer service with them? At The Ritz-Carlton, the small, laminated card containing the basic service practices is considered part of every employee's uniform. It is a written set of standards and behavior, as they pertain to dealing with guests, that were introduced in 1983 under the leadership of Horst Schulze. Called the "Gold Standards," they are found on the card.

First are written The Ritz-Carlton motto and credo. As you already know, the hotel's motto is "We are Ladies and Gentlemen serving Ladies and Gentlemen." The credo consists of three statements:

1. "The Ritz-Carlton Hotel is a place where genuine care and comfort of our guests is our highest mission."

2. "We pledge to provide the finest personal service and facilities for our guests, who will always enjoy a warm, relaxed, yet refined ambience."

3. "The Ritz-Carlton experience enlivens the senses, instills well-being, and fulfills even the unexpressed wishes and needs of our guests."

The three steps of service are described as:

1. "Give a warm and sincere greeting. Use the guest's name if and when possible."

2. "Anticipate and comply with guest needs."

3. "Bid a fond farewell. Give guests a warm good-bye and use their names, if and when possible."

The Ritz-Carlton "basics" comprise a definitive list of guidelines that provide clear instructions for employees in dealing with their guests. For example, one of these reads, "Be an ambassador of your hotel in and outside of the workplace. Always talk positively. Communicate any concerns to the appropriate person."

The employee promise is also found on the card. It reads, "The Ritz-Carlton considers its staff the most important resource in providing service to its guests. Promises it makes to its staff include the following:

- "By applying the principles of trust, honesty, respect, integrity, and commitment, we nurture and maximize talent to the benefit of each individual and the company.

- "The Ritz-Carlton fosters a work environment where diversity is values, quality of life is enhanced, individual aspirations are fulfilled, and The Ritz-Carlton mystique is strengthened."

Are you willing to make those promises, those commitments to your employees as well as to your customers? How would you like to work for a company that is willing to do that?

By the way, since its inception in 1988, 58 companies have been awarded the prestigious Malcolm Baldrige National Quality Award. Many consider this to be the highest award offered to companies in customer service. The Ritz-Carlton has won it twice.

THE RITZ-CARLTON MODEL

I have interviewed an executive from The Ritz-Carlton on my radio show a few times. He not only believes in the Ritz-Carlton model of service, but he loves to talk about it.

He describes one of the practices of The Ritz-Carlton as "making a bigger cookie." He says that most companies find ways to make more profits by cutting back. They figure out ways to put fewer raisins in the box or fewer chips in the cookies. At The Ritz-Carlton, they figure out how to make the cookie bigger and sell it for more.

He also shared the story of the high scores The Ritz-Carlton in San Francisco had for making guests feel welcome, while the Buckhead (Georgia) Ritz-Carlton had lower scores in the category. Closer investigation revealed that the customer contact employees in San Francisco wore earpieces and could communicate to each other, thus letting others know when guests were arriving and sending along names and other information as it was gathered. When the Buckhead location adopted this method, its customer scores increased quickly. This relentless effort to make customers feel important is one of the many lessons learned from the Ritz-Carlton model of service.

Bruce Seigel, who is an area marketing director with The Ritz-Carlton, is clear that people make the difference at The Ritz-Carlton. "We don't hire, we select," said Seigel in a 2004 interview in the *Atlanta Business Chronicle*. "I can teach anyone to make soup, cut lemons, or serve a drink, but I can't teach people to be warm, genuine, friendly and kind. So we identify those talents in the individuals we hire because our brand stands for that kind of care and comfort. If you don't select those kinds of people, no matter what kind of training you give them, that care and comfort won't come out in a genuine way."

As part of the selection process, The Ritz-Carlton prospective hires go through an intensive assessment of their attitudes, including evaluations of such categories as self-esteem, positivity, empathy, and caring. Once selected, employees attend a rigorous three-day orientation prior to going into the field for their assignments. Following a stint in their permanent locations, they are brought back to repeat the orientation. This serves two functions. First, it reinforces the Ritz-Carlton standards to the still-new employee. Second, it gives the new employee an opportunity to have observed whether the field employees are actually practicing the techniques taught at orientation. (Hint: They are.)

Talking to Ritz-Carlton employees is always interesting; their constant references to The Ritz-Carlton's "ladies and gentlemen" reflect the seriousness and sincerity with which the company takes its philosophy of respect for both guests and fellow employees. Each time I speak with an employee of The Ritz-Carlton, I see clearly the impact that this simple practice of constantly showing respect for others can have on an organization.

The Ritz-Carlton Standard: The Ritz-Carlton sets the standard for keeping customer service uppermost in the mind of each and every employee. From the top of the organization, the standard of emphasis on quality is made clear to everyone in the company. Ask any Ritz-Carlton employee how often they talk about customer service, and you get the same response: "Every day."

The Ritz-Carlton Challenge: The challenge offered by The Ritz-Carlton is this: How often do *your* employees discuss the methods practiced to serve your customers? How often do *you* talk about it with them? Is it at the semiannual meeting when you bring in a speaker like me to "motivate" your employees? (If so, it won't work.) Is it after you've lost a major customer due to indifference or lack of empowerment because someone didn't act quickly enough because they didn't know that they could? I challenge you to talk with your employees every day . . . every day.

CHAPTER SIX

WHEN *CUSTOMERS* CALL IN SICK

""*Good Enough Never Is*"**"**
—DEBBI FIELDS

THERE ARE A LOT of well-known names in Memphis. Mike Rose is one. He is the retired chairman of Harrah's Corporation, an active civic leader, and a dedicated University of Memphis alumnus. He has provided leadership in many aspects of the city's success and is well worthy of all of the press and praise he receives. Harrah's quietly made a one-million-dollar donation to the University of Memphis when he retired. One of the largest youth soccer complexes in the Mid-South bears his name.

Mike's wife, Debbi, does not have the same name recognition, but she is a pretty well-known figure in her own right, both in Memphis and throughout the rest of the country. People listen when she speaks about her business experiences. You may be wondering, *Who is Debbi Rose?* You know her as Mrs. Fields.

That's right—the cookie lady—the one who created the legendary cookies. Her story is indeed the stuff of legends, but the Mrs. Fields story also teaches much about the never-ending quest for customer service excellence and the fundamental truth I was learning along the way. It is what is at the core of the company that determines that way in which customers get treated. What goes on within a company is just as important as the product that goes out. I like this story a lot.

FINDING MRS. FIELDS

Not being much of a sweets eater, I wasn't familiar with Mrs. Fields's cookies or anyone else's for that matter. Finding Mrs. Fields and her cookies was an unexpected discovery in my quest for the best service providers.

I was asked to speak at a breakfast meeting of a local business association. As we were finalizing the details of my engagement, my contact told me how excited they were to have me speaking to their group (always a good thing to hear!). Then, he said how much they had been "knocked out" by the previous month's speaker. (This is not the best thing to hear—you generally prefer to follow someone who was less than a "knockout.")

I learned that the previous speaker was Debbi Fields Rose. My client raved about how powerful her message was. He enthusiastically described the Mrs. Fields story and the impact it had on the attendees at the session. I paid close attention to what I was hearing and started to ask around and see what the fuss was about. I found out it was about a lot.

FOLLOWING YOUR PASSION

When Debbi Fields decided twenty-five years ago to sell cookies for a living, having had what she calls a "passion" for cookies as a child, she was missing only four ingredients (pun intended). They were: (1) education, (2) business experience, (3) any kind of encouragement from her family, and (4) money. Other than that, Debbi was ready to go into business.

"I knew my disadvantages," she said in a speech reported in the *Huntsville Item* ("Mrs. Fields Gives Recipe for Success," by Emilie Hornack, July 14, 2004). "I was young, had no college credentials, and came from little means. I was blonde, and people figured I had no brains. Growing up, my sisters nicknamed me 'Stupid.' I love them dearly, and I know that happens in big families, but I really struggled with that and had a lot of self-doubt."

Debbi's father, however, had taught her that success is not about money but that it is about loving what you do. She grew up being called the "cookie girl." She loved making cookies; she made them whenever she could. She even used her salary from her first job (the first female foul-ball girl for the Oakland Athletics) to buy butter, vanilla, and chocolate chips to make cookies.

Debbi Fields Rose knows what her work is all about. "Since I was a little girl," she said, "I've believed I was put here to make people smile. I know it sounds like the silliest thing, but that's what I think I've ended up doing with my life in this business—making people smile."

Starting with this passion for her product and the desire to make people happy, Debbi built a wonderful and successful company.

ONE COOKIE AT A TIME

In the beginning, the more people tried to convince Debbi that a cookie business would never work, the more determined she became. After all, these same people had been eating her cookies for years! Even her then-husband, Randy, didn't think she could do it. Still, he gave Debbi his support, and together they were rejected by numerous banks before finally getting a loan to open a store.

By noon on her first day of business—August 16, 1977—at

Debbi's Chocolate Chippery in Palo Alto, California, it was beginning to look like all the naysayers were right. Debbi had not
sold one cookie! So she went out on the street and started giving
her cookies away, and soon people were coming in to buy them.

"Randy had made a bet that I couldn't make $50 in sales that
first day, but I did," Debbi is quoted as saying. (Marilyn Sadler,
"Baking a Name for Herself," *Memphis Magazine,* June 1999.)
"What emerged from that was setting goals in increments. If
goals are within reach, they don't look so daunting."

She took that basic lesson and developed a management
process around it. Basically, she took large tasks and began to
break them down into bite-sized pieces (another pun intended).
"It's all tied to a very simple principle that's called 'hour-by-
hour management,'" she says, "and today colleges use it as a
case study in business efficiency."

Today, Mrs. Fields has grown into a 1,600-location franchise
empire. *Something* has got to be different to get this many people
to go into a store to buy cookies. If there were ever a basic com-
modity, cookies have to be it. After all, how many ways can a
cookie be made? Every mom I have ever known has had a "secret" recipe for the best cookie ever made. What I found was
that Debbi Fields had a secret recipe (she'll reveal it later on in
this chapter), and it did make the difference.

IS GOOD ENOUGH GOOD ENOUGH FOR YOU?

The "cookie girl" never sat back and rested on her laurels. She
wasn't just going to make cookies and sell them. She was going
to make the best cookie she possibly could. She kept working to
improve her cookie recipe. "I found out how much butter I
could put in them before it was too much. I found out how
much chocolate I could put in the dough before the dough

wouldn't hold any more," Debbi said in her speech. "I took the cookies to the extreme."

Mrs. Fields made a cookie that almost no one could compete with. Part of the process was keeping only the freshest cookies on the shelf. "Any cookie that sat on the shelf for two hours became an orphan cookie and they were donated to charities or sent home with people," she said.

Debbi came up with new ways to get customers into her stores, even to the extent of pumping the fresh smells out into the malls where the stores were located. Mall shoppers would be hit with the aroma of fresh-baked cookies. Who could refuse?

Debbi learned customers' names and made sure that shopping at her store was a fun experience. She always tried to give customers the sense that they were having a good time. Today, she says that she knew that she really had something when *customers* would call in sick—to let her know they wouldn't be in that day. Talk about owning your customers!

As the popularity and number of her stores grew, so did her determination to provide the same customer experience at multiple stores as she did when her company was small. She once dropped in on one of her stores and tasted a cookie. She noticed that something wasn't right and asked the store manager what he thought. The manager said it was good enough. "Good enough never is," she replied.

MIXING BUSINESS WITH CUSTOMER SERVICE

Debbi knew that she would continue to strive for the highest standards for her product while still understanding what her business was about. "I am in the feel-good feeling business," she said in her speech. "My job makes people feel good."

Mrs. Fields consistently delivers a top-notch product and is one of the best service providers around. By keeping her eye on these goals, Debbi developed a highly successful business model, one that has been studied and copied by many other companies.

In addition to employing the hour-by-hour management process discussed earlier, Mrs. Fields was one of the first companies to use technology to jump-start its retail growth. Debbi Fields led her company into the technology age, enhancing operations and production with a state-of-the-art computer system. Her program is used as a model for business efficiency at Harvard Business School. Today, it is still used as an example of combining sound business practices with technology.

Sound business practice notwithstanding, Debbi Fields today will share her most valuable tip to describe her success. "The secret ingredient has always been love. I mean, that's what, you know, I put in the product." (Marilyn Sadler, "Baking a Name for Herself," *Memphis Magazine,* June 1999.)

The Mrs. Fields Standard: Very few companies reflect the ability to both create a customer-friendly atmosphere and do business as well as Mrs. Fields. Imagine having customers call in sick! What does that say about their treatment? Making customers feel important enough that they think they will be missed is the absolute elimination of indifference in a workplace and perhaps one of the most sincere compliments that a company can be paid.

The Mrs. Fields Challenge: Are your customers calling in when they are sick? I don't mean this literally, but do you make your customers feel so important to your company that they feel they would be missed if they left you? If the answer to this is "No," you're just renting them; you don't own them. When some other company makes them feel important, they'll drop you and go to where they feel important—where they'll feel like calling in when they're sick.

CHAPTER SEVEN

EXTRAORDINARY EMPLOYEE EMPOWERMENT

*"Rule #1—Use your good judgment in all
situations. There will be no additional rules."*
—THE NORDSTROM EMPLOYEE HANDBOOK

NOT HAVING A NORDSTROM in my city, I have not had the experience of shopping there. However, this name kept coming up over and over as I was on my quest. Other people repeatedly told me about *their* Nordstrom experiences. My sister Laura asked more than once, "Are you writing about Nordstrom?" The wife of a good friend raved about going to New York and shopping at Nordstrom.

I've never set foot in Nordstrom, have never seen a Nordstrom ad, nor heard the Nordstrom jingle. I don't have to. I have the Internet.

FIRST IMPRESSIONS

I was not overly impressed with Nordstrom's website. I usually like to find something a little more "passionate" about a company's commitment to customer service, especially those with values coming from their founders. I didn't find any of this on Nordstrom's website, but I *did* find the fact that it makes it easy to return items that are purchased either in the store or over the Internet. This impressed me.

What began to impress me more, though, were the responses from Nordstrom customers who would tell me stories when I asked about their shopping experiences. I started by asking members of my audiences when I spoke. I even solicited Nordstrom stories on my website. They were small stories, not overwhelming instances of earth-shattering service, but they revealed a consistency of courtesy and customer interest that meant much to the folks experiencing it. Something was different about Nordstrom, just as with the other companies I was studying.

What I heard began to sound quite interesting to me. The following is typical of what I was told or written:

> "I shopped at a Nordstrom and bought a couple of hundred dollars worth of merchandise. It was certainly not a large purchase to them, but significant to me. A couple of days later, I got a handwritten note from the sales clerk thanking me for my purchase and for shopping at Nordstrom. It was not printed with just a signature; it was completely handwritten. I am impressed, to say the least."

THE LEGEND OF THE TIRE PURCHASE

You won't spend much time researching Nordstrom without running across the story of an elderly man who went to a Nordstrom store and complained that the tires that he had bought there were bad and that he wanted his money back. This is not an unusual customer service story until you find out that Nordstrom doesn't sell tires!

The sales clerk politely explained that fact, but the man persisted with his complaint, assuring the clerk that he had indeed purchased his tires there and that he wanted a refund. After a few minutes of the conversation, the Nordstrom clerk refunded the man's money.

You can understand why this has become a legendary story in customer service. While the exact details are not known, the fact remains that the story lives not because it is unbelievable, but because it *is* believable. It sounds like something that a Nordstrom employee would do.

I spoke recently to the annual meeting of a group of hotel executives. During my talk, I told one of the Nordstrom stories that I like to use when I speak. At the break, one of the executives approached me and told me that her company had hosted a meeting of Nordstrom managers at one of its hotels. She first told me how polite and kind the Nordstrom group was, which was exactly what she had expected. Then she said that she had asked some of them whether the "tire legend" was true. She was assured that it was.

One interesting exercise is to reverse this tire legend to reflect what would have happened if this had been *your* customer and *your* employee. What would have happened? Would your employees have done the same thing? Would they be fearful of what would happen to them when it became known? Would they have been reprimanded, fired, fined, or praised? What would *you* have done if *you* had been the clerk?

HOW THICK IS YOUR HANDBOOK?

What really blew me away was when someone told me about the Nordstrom employee handbook. I am a skeptic about employee handbooks for the most part, believing that they are rarely read. I often ask members of my audiences whether their company has an employee handbook and, if so, how long it is and whether they know its contents. Most respond to these questions with "Thick" and "No," respectively.

I "Googled" the Nordstrom employee handbook and received 9,170 reference points. What I found was both incredible and easily verified.

Each Nordstrom employee receives the employee handbook. It consists of *one page* and reads as follows:

> Welcome to Nordstrom. We're glad to have you with our company. Our number one goal is to provide outstanding customer service. Set both your personal and professional goals high. We have great confidence in your ability to achieve them. Nordstrom rules: Rule #1—Use your good judgment in all situations. There will be no additional rules. Please feel free to ask your department manager, store manager or division general manager any question at any time.

That is it—that is the whole thing! What this leads to is a group of highly empowered employees at Nordstrom who are free to make decisions based upon their own judgment as to the best way to serve their customers.

The more I talked about Nordstrom, the more intrigued I became. I began to mention it during talks I gave, and the nodding heads in my audiences (especially the women) always got my attention.

When I said how much I enjoyed the Nordstrom jingle, I would notice the looks of puzzlement on my audience. (That's because it doesn't have one.) I would mention that I like the Nordstrom slogan (again, it doesn't have one), and my audience would try to remember it. When I spoke about the Nordstrom logo (once again, there is no such thing), nobody knew what it looked like. All Nordstrom has for advertising is a reputation for world-class service.

THE INVERTED PYRAMID

Perhaps the most in-depth research done regarding Nordstrom and its service philosophies is Robert Spector's book *The Nordstrom Way* (New York: John Wiley & Sons, 1999). In his book, Spector tells stories that deal with the extraordinary empowerment that Nordstrom employees have in dealing with customers, how they feel free to make decisions for their customers on behalf of Nordstrom without fear of management disapproval. "Nordstrom would rather leave it up to me to decide what is best," states one Nordstrom employee. This empowerment is probably the most well-known aspect of the Nordstrom culture because it the most easily noticed among customers.

Spector further explains the organization of Nordstrom as an "inverted pyramid." By this, he explains that the top of the organization, the widest base, is occupied by customers. The pyramid then descends to sales/support employees, department managers, and on through to executives, the chairman, and the board of directors. It is the exact opposite of the traditional organization chart. In the Nordstrom chart, the entire workings of the organization support the sales department. "The only thing we have going for us is the way we take care of our customers," explained Ray Johnson, retired cochairman, "and the people who take care of the customers are on the floor."

Nordstrom constantly reinforces the notion that employees should be left to use their best judgment. The philosophy is that if given enough room to make decisions on their own, employees will make decisions in the best interest of the company.

HIRE THE SMILE, TEACH THE SKILL

The hiring philosophy at Nordstrom helps to explain the success of the chain. Nordstrom does not place emphasis on experience in retail. It feels that anyone can be taught this. It believes that it is more difficult to learn the right attitude. So, it has adopted the adage "Hire the smile, teach the skill." In other words, hire those with the right people skills and attitude and teach them how to do their jobs, as opposed to following the methods of most companies.

The overwhelming majority of companies emphasize experience in their hiring processes. They put much, perhaps too much, emphasis on knowledge of the job, assuming that this will cost less money in the long term. After all, less training has to mean less expense, doesn't it? What they miss is the fact that emphasis on skill, rather than attitude, can result in hiring mistakes and even greater turnover. Companies are hiring people with such poor attitudes that, in spite of their on-the-job experience, their service suffers. Their indifferent or poor service leads to unhappy customers, and that surely will have a negative impact on the bottom line.

Nordstrom is looking for people who are *already* nice and *already* motivated, because the company provides little in the way of a formalized training program. The company is not necessarily looking for people with previous retail experience, because those people have already learned to say, "No" to the customer. Nordstrom doesn't want them to say, "No"— Nordstrom wants them to say, "Yes." The company's preference is to hire a nice person and teach her how to sell, rather than hire a saleswoman and teach her how to be nice.

Bruce Nordstrom was once asked who *really* trains the salespeople. His answer was: "Their parents."

ISN'T EMPOWERING YOUR EMPLOYEES RISKY?

Empowerment might be the most difficult process to implement in customer service, because it means you have to fully trust in the judgment of employees. Many executives consider empowering employees to be too risky, the same as satisfaction guarantees. They fear it because it is too easy to abuse and too difficult to manage. This is a shame, because employee empowerment is also the key to world-class service.

The companies that "get it" (like the ones discussed in this book) constantly reflect this idea of empowerment. It makes no difference whether you have one or 1,000 employees. Empowerment means making each of them feel that he or she is important to your team, and giving them roles in which they have some freedom to operate, to make decisions on their own that are consistent with advancing your corporate values. It means giving your employees the power to do their jobs. However, it also involves trusting each of your employees, which is something that many employers are not ready to do.

Statements of trust don't get much stronger than the one in the Nordstrom employee handbook: "Use your best judgment at all times." Ask yourself this question: Would that be enough instruction for *your* employees? Would you leave for a month with that being all you instructed your employees to do?

It might be appropriate to mention here what empowerment is *not*. It is *not* giving away the store to make a customer happy. It *is* using good judgment, supported by the company, to do whatever is reasonable to make a customer happy, understanding that occasionally this is going to lose the company money. The companies that "get it" understand that this is money they will get back over the long term from loyal customers.

DISEMPOWERED EMPLOYEES AT WORK

How many times have you found a problem with something you use or own? You determined the problem, looked up the telephone number for the customer service department, and made the call. After getting through the maze to finally talk to someone, you identify yourself and explain your problem. Have you ever then been asked to hold, and then been transferred to someone else, only to have to start over with everything? If you answered, "Yes," you are among the millions who experience this frustrating example of lack of empowerment every day. No one wants to experience this situation, but far too many companies allow it to happen all the time What these companies don't realize is that they must have an empowered work force to provide outstanding service.

Let's look at another, hypothetical example of the lack of empowerment.

You purchase a PDA from a well-known electrical store. A sales rep helps you out; you give him your credit card and go home with the PDA. Excited with your new purchase, you get home and notice a scratch on the screen of the PDA. It is not major, but it's a flaw nonetheless.

You return to the store and find the sales rep. You tell him about your problem. Instead of exchanging the product, you offer to take a partial refund and keep the scratched PDA. This is a perfectly legitimate request, which will save you some money, but also allow for your inconvenience. The store will keep the sale (even if for a bit less money), avoid the hassle of returning the product, and create a happy customer in the process. The sales rep says he'll have to check with his manager, but that he thinks this is reasonable. He doesn't have the authority to make this happen, he explains. (It should be noted here that if the rep had been empowered, the deal could have been made, and you would be out the door and on your way home while the sales rep helped another customer.)

The sales rep comes back in a few minutes with a department manager. The manager is polite and asks you to repeat your situation to her. You go through the story again, and the manager agrees that this is reasonable, but she needs to check with the store manager to make the deal.

The store manager is located, comes hurriedly to greet you, asks you to explain the situation again, and asks for your receipt. He says the offer is reasonable but that he has never done it before. He asks whether you're sure you don't just want to exchange the product, and you say, "No."

The store manager explains that he will have to call "somebody" and get approval to do this. It is a fair deal, one that you want, but the store manager has to get approval.

Finally, after a long wait, the store manager returns with approval and instructions. You get a partial refund and leave the store, thinking it is the last time you will shop there. Your time has been wasted, the salesperson's time has been wasted, management's time has been wasted, other customers have been made to wait, and they've lost you as a customer. Not a very good outcome.

If the sales rep operated in an empowered environment, he either would know what the policy is for this example *or* would feel comfortable making the refund and explaining it to his manager later, in order to learn what should be done the next time.

EMPOWERMENT AND VALUES

Empowerment and values go hand in hand. The basic premise of trusting employees to do the right thing comes directly from the amount of trust that can be placed in their judgment. This is why the Nordstrom model is so significant: the emphasis being on the use of good judgment in all situations. The fact that employees are empowered with that trust from the first day of employment tells the entire story.

One of my favorite guests on my talk show has been author John Miller. John wrote *The Question Behind the Question* (G.P. Putnam's Sons, NY, 2004). He raises the issue of what he calls an "integrity test" and challenges all employees of an organization to ask themselves whether they believe in the integrity and principles of their organization. He suggests that they reflect on what they say at home to family and friends about the company for which they work.

As if that were not challenging enough, Miller goes further to suggest that employees have a decision to make at that time. He calls it "believe or leave." In other words, if you do not have respect for your employer and what the company is all about, you should leave—as soon as possible.

SERVICE IS NOT ALWAYS FUN

It is only fair to point out here that while Nordstrom is renowned for its relentless pursuit of customer service excellence, it is also known for its competitive atmosphere among sales reps and their undeniable pressure to maintain customer satisfaction. Goals are set and constantly measured, and employees must meet their goals. There are certain employees who cannot stand up to the constant pressure of the quest for excellence. In the Nordstrom environment, individuals who cannot compete and attain their goals are slowly weeded out. This results in only the very finest employees surviving and customers receiving only the best in service.

Read this from the Nordstrom website: "Our founder, John W. Nordstrom, believed in a simple philosophy: Listen to the customer. Provide them with what they want. Appreciate the fact they came to your store, and do everything within your power to ensure that they're satisfied when they leave."

The Nordstrom Standard: No slogan, no jingle, no logo—simply a reputation for taking care of its customers. Perhaps no company sets a standard for employee empowerment like Nordstrom. "Use your best judgment in all situations." That is the only rule. What other company makes it clearer that the number-one criteria for a good employee is to do the right thing all the time? Many other companies might give this generalized instruction to their employees . . . why not? The difference is that at Nordstrom they trust their employees to do it.

The Nordstrom Challenge: This one is going to be tough. Are you ready to turn the keys to the vault over to your employees? Are you ready to let them make the decisions to keep your customers? Are you willing to leave your company for a week, a month, and be comfortable that things will be run based upon the values that are in place? If you answer, "No," you have the wrong values, the wrong people, or both.

CHAPTER EIGHT

ABSOLUTELY, POSITIVELY: THE PURSUIT OF PERFECTION

"*If you want to be a great leader, find a big parade and run in front of it.*"
—POGO (AS QUOTED BY FRED SMITH)

I HAD A FEELING that my search for the top customer service companies would wind up sooner or later at FedEx. Call me a "homer" if you like, but no Memphian would consider not including this company in their list of "the best." From national awards (including the prestigious Malcolm Baldrige National Quality Award) to recognition as one of the best places to work, FedEx reflects its values consistently.

I personally know dozens of FedEx employees. I don't know any who aren't proud of where they work. Although FedEx Corp. has several subsidiaries, all of them focus on one thing above all: 100 percent customer satisfaction. In fact, one of the company's original slogans was, "When it absolutely, positively has to get there overnight." That's sending an unmistakably clear message to customers and one that shouldn't be sent without a process to back it up.

MR. SMITH GOES TO MEMPHIS

The concept for Federal Express originated in a graduate paper written by Yale student Fred Smith. Smith wrote about the routing system that other airfreight companies were then using. Contrary to what many think, Smith didn't "invent" the airfreight industry, he simply moved it to a more effective level. Federal Express originally operated out of Little Rock, Arkansas, but the first packages were flown out of Memphis in 1973. According to the company website, 186 packages were delivered to 25 cities that first night. That number now exceeds 3 million every night.

The company moved to Memphis, due in part to both its geographical location and the fact that the airport rarely closed because of weather. The economic impact that FedEx has on this city is considerable, as the company employs an estimated 30,000 in Memphis.

STRIVING FOR 100 PERCENT
CUSTOMER SATISFACTION

Its dedication to service and quality has been the most important element in the company's success. To further explore that philosophy, I decided that I would directly contact someone from the corporate office at FedEx rather than relying on my friends who work there. I wanted to get the corporate perspective on the pride of the service provided.

I was referred to the FedEx Manager's Guide, which includes its corporate mission statement as well as descriptions of the corporate commitment to quality. The FedEx mission statement, as found on its website, is as follows:

> FedEx will produce superior financial returns for shareowners
> by providing high value-added supply chain, transportation,

business and related information services through focused operating companies. Customer requirements will be met in the highest quality manner appropriate to each market segment served. FedEx will strive to develop mutually rewarding relationships with its employees, partners and suppliers. Safety will be the first consideration in all operations. Corporate activities will be conducted to the highest ethical and professional standards.

The commitment to quality is not taken lightly by FedEx and it is reflected in the stories of excellent service provided by its employees.

A FedEx corporate manager explained to me the philosophy as stated in the FedEx Manager's Guide—that FedEx instills in managers, who must then instill the same commitment in front line employees, that service is more than just talk at FedEx; it is a reason for being. It makes no difference where the service is provided around the world, FedEx's goal is the same—100 percent customer satisfaction. It is this 100 percent commitment on the part of each employee that separates FedEx from its competition. Its employees are given opportunities every day to make differences in people's lives. FedEx doesn't take this lightly. These opportunities come in the form of making sure a wedding dress is delivered on time. Or perhaps a critical computer part, a life-saving machine, or even an important business document. Whatever it might be, the mission is to get it delivered . . . on time . . . every time.

FedEx invests heavily in training, communications, the quality process, and information systems to achieve this result. More vital than all of these massive investments, however, is the commitment of each individual FedEx Express employee to this 100 percent standard. Few commercial ventures demand such faultless execution and teamwork.

The Manager's Guide states that it is vital that every FedEx manager and employee understand the importance of service—it is described as the "lifeblood" of FedEx. It is emphasized that FedEx strives for a service standard of 100 percent. Nothing less is acceptable. It may be for other companies, but not for FedEx. It is this pursuit that causes employees to give extra, knowing it is the corporate way.

EMPLOYEE AWARDS

FedEx Express employees live the values that have been identified as core to the company's philosophy. They are:

Respect—Treat each person with dignity and respect.

Integrity—Be worthy of trust.

Service—Serve others.

Excellence—Relentlessly strive to exceed expectations.

Communication—Understand and be understood.

There are hundreds of stories of employees who have gone "above and beyond" to provide extraordinary service to customers. Many are recognized at an annual recognition banquet and presented an award. The award is given to employees who go above and beyond normal job expectations to provide superior customer service. Winners take the recognition seriously and with a great deal of pride. Here are three examples:

James C. Amrine, **Courier:** On Saturday, May 24, 2003, a customer who had a package marked "Hold for Pick-up" at the Montrose station arrived after the station had already closed. The package contained a film, which had been advertised for two weeks prior to that date. The film's director was scheduled to introduce the film at 7 p.m. that evening. Alerted by the customer to the situation, FedEx customer service contacted James, who drove to the station and found the package. Although James was not on duty, he used his personal vehicle to drive 65 miles and successfully delivered the package before the 7 p.m. deadline.

Oscar E. Bernal, **Manager, Station Operations:** One Friday afternoon, the FedEx station in Cancun received a frantic call from a customer. He desperately needed his package, which contained his passport, because he was leaving on Sunday. Oscar volunteered to deliver the passport personally the next day, even though the station does not offer Saturday delivery. The next day, Oscar discovered that the recipient's location was a remote hotel situated in the jungle. Undeterred, Oscar successfully delivered the package by driving several hours on unpaved road, dodging gaping potholes and screeching monkeys.

Vincent Bruno, **Ramp Agent, and** *John S. Crawford,* **Senior Operations Support Specialist:** FedEx operations in S. Florida was informed on a Friday that the bridge connecting Sanibel Island to mainland Florida would be closed the following Monday for emergency repairs. As a result, the Fort Myers station would not be able to make deliveries on that day as all packages destined for Sanibel were normally transported over the bridge. Even though Vincent and John were on vacation, they volunteered their time and boat services to transport couriers and packages to prearranged waiting FedEx delivery vans. Vincent and Bruno continued to transport couriers and packages back and forth all day to and from the island, helping maintain on-time delivery for over 200 packages.

WHAT ABSOLUTELY, POSITIVELY MEANS

Since its inception in 1973, FedEx has had one goal: to provide 100 percent customer satisfaction. Two things have been consistent since that time. The first is that the goal has never changed. Not once. The second is that the company has never attained its goal. Not once.

This goal is the cornerstone of the company's success. It is not perfection that places FedEx at the top of its industry but the relentless pursuit of that perfection, which reinforces a desire to be the most reliable company in its industry. That it never gives up the quest for perfection is what separates it from all others. This is a trademark that any company should emulate.

The ongoing quest for "perfect package delivery" has led to the most sophisticated package-tracking system in the industry. Customers are actually invited to watch the company's progress in handling their packages during transit! How many companies actually invite customers to watch as a product is produced? Does yours?

WANTED: EXECUTIVES WHO "GET IT"

I read with interest a *Business Week Online* article (Joan O'C. Hamilton, "Quick, FedEx Me an Executive," May 17, 1999) that described the companies in Silicon Valley as ranking in the "don't get it" category when it comes to customer service. However, the author went on to state that this was changing, in part due to the recruitment of FedEx executives to leadership positions. The reason for hiring these people is their experience of working within a culture based on "making customers happy."

The author describes the executive pool at FedEx as a "gold mine." Interestingly enough, the article suggests that the recruitment of leadership was not a dramatic problem for FedEx because it had so much talent in place to fill the recruited voids. The outstanding culture of service bred new leaders to replace those who left.

The FedEx Standard: The continual quest for 100 percent customer satisfaction. Employees at all levels have gone way beyond normal expectations to meet these goals. However, the reputation of FedEx as a leader in reliability is based as much on its effort to resolve problems as it is on its success ratio. If a delivery doesn't go as planned, the company makes a dedicated effort to correct the situation as quickly as possible.

The FedEx Challenge: I challenge your company to review its focus and to determine whether it is willing to go the extra mile to satisfy customers when there are problems. Perfection is impossible, but relentless service is attainable. In doing this, you'll have happier customers and happier employees as well.

CHAPTER NINE

A PLACE WHERE KINDNESS GROWS

"Two are better than one; because they have a good reward for their labor. For if they fall, the one will lift up his fellow: but woe to him that is alone when he falleth; for he hath not another to help him up."
—ECCLESIASTES 4:9–10

AS A SPIRITUAL PERSON, I like to think that things happen for a reason. I don't really believe in coincidences; I prefer to think in terms of bigger things. That being said, I found great interest in a local news column that briefly mentioned one of FedEx's outsourcing companies receiving the highest customer service honor that FedEx awards. I wanted to find out a little more about the type of company that, first, could be hired by FedEx and that, second, could perform at a level that would result in being given a customer service award by such a top service provider.

I read the article closely and recognized a prominent name: Baddour. There is a successful retail store, Fred's, that is principally controlled by the prominent Baddour family and operates 530 stores in the Southeastern part of the country. I assumed that FedEx had some relationship with them. I was wrong.

THE BADDOUR CENTER

The Baddour referred to in the column was indeed the same Baddour family, but this particular operation had nothing to do with the retail operation. Rather, it was the Baddour Center, a 120-acre campus-home for adults with mild or moderate mental retardation. One of the Baddours, Paul, donated his home in Senatobia, Mississippi, to be used to house and care for five people, one of whom was a family member. His generosity now has grown into this beautiful, multi-building facility that provides opportunity for these residents to enjoy friendship and to accomplish goals in all facets of life. The number of individuals residing and working there now totals over 170. It is a beautiful, special place.

Part of the opportunity offered to the residents comes in the form of vocational work. Operating from "The People Factory," one such program offers fulfillment services for companies on an outsourced basis. Around fifteen years ago, the parent of one of the residents at the Baddour Center mentioned the work being done there to a FedEx executive. Following casual conversation and a review of services, FedEx decided that it would use some of the Baddour Center's personnel to outsource some of its work.

The People Factory has grown to become the operation that it is today, which involves more than 50 employees who are dedicated to supporting FedEx and are receiving award after award for outstanding service to customers.

I thought that taking a closer look at this enterprise might be of interest, considering the timing and angle, so I contacted the columnist who had written the article for the *Commercial Appeal*, Jane Roberts, and asked whom I could talk to at the Baddour Center. She graciously gave me the name of the person in charge of public relations, who just as graciously welcomed my request for a tour.

I drove the forty-or-so miles south to the center. I walked in and met Kerry, Steve, and Christi, who agreed to show me around. We went directly to the fulfillment area, and I was invited to look around and ask anything I wanted to anyone working there. I took them up on their offer and began to look around and stroll through the facility.

WHAT I FOUND

I have been speaking and writing on customer service for years. I have been involved in consulting projects that involved customer loyalty and retention. I'm going to tell you right now that I have never encountered a place where the basic concepts of customer service, the underlying principles, are so inherently practiced as at the Baddour Center. If you need to "fix" your customer service operations, you need to go there with a bucket and bring back everything you can in the way of attitude, pride, and trust.

Most companies will tell you that the first contact with a new customer is the most important. This will usually form the basis of the opinion that that customer will maintain for a long time—perhaps forever. Assuming that this is true, FedEx must put a lot of trust in the work being done at the Baddour Center.

I learned quickly that every welcome package that goes to new FedEx customers in the United States is put together there. Every single one! And I noticed right away the complex machinery being used. This is not a group of people who are licking and stuffing envelopes.

I also learned that these packages are personalized to either the company or the individual to whom they are sent, with over 200 possible iterations. This leads to the creation of over 35 million new airbills a year being created in addition to the thousands of packages that are assembled to welcome new customers.

I strolled around the facility and found that I was welcomed by, and introduced to, several of the workers. They noticed me as they worked; they anticipated my approach. They would begin to smile as I got near, and almost giggle when I would begin to speak. To a person, they would tell me their name and describe with great pride what they did and how it fit into the big scheme of getting these important packages out to "our customers." I honestly felt that if I had a critical package that needed to get somewhere, I couldn't think of safer, more caring hands than these for that package to be placed in. FedEx obviously feels the same way; getting the welcome package out quickly is an important part of the company's stellar customer service.

I found it interesting to note that there was a warehouse of printed material that was used to put together the welcome packages. I saw shelves and shelves, literally hundreds of thousands of dollars worth of paper products. It was explained to me that FedEx originally sent someone out to check on the inventory once a week, just to make sure it was taken care of. That's probably not a bad idea when dealing with their huge amount of product. Today, they check it only twice a year—because it's obviously in good hands.

KINDNESS AT THE CORE

Something was becoming very clear to me as I continued to stroll around the facility. First of all, there was a great deal of trust that had been put into these people from both their employer and its customer, FedEx. Second, it was clear that the work was done with pride and dignity. Every employee I visited spoke with pride of his or her work and talked about how it fit into the big picture. Most measurable was the kindness. From the way I (an unannounced visitor) was welcomed to the support that they showed for each other, it was incredible.

It was described in the Baddour Center's annual report like this: "What emerges from this small volume with poignant clarity is an affirmation of life's most precious treasures: love, compassion, understanding, faith, patience in adversity, and the real meaning of family."

At one point during my visit, I saw a couple of ladies standing next to each other, looking at a sophisticated piece of machinery. One had a look of angst, the other looked calm. The calm one had her arm on the other's shoulder. "I broke this," explained the first lady. "I'm fixing it," replied the second, with a kind smile.

As I drove back from this award-winning company, I reflected on the good feeling I had during my visit. Not about me, mind you. I was the recipient there, not the donor. I had done nothing except receive, that morning, but I felt good.

I knew then that I had found what had made me feel so special when I called L.L.Bean, when I went to Chick-fil-A's headquarters, when I toured St. Jude. What I had found was kindness. The kindness in that place was contagious, and it made me feel good. Unfortunately, this kind of experience happens in too few companies.

What's needed is a kindness revolution.

CHAPTER TEN

KINDNESS: STARTING THE REVOLUTION

"*Kind words can be short and easy to speak but their echoes are truly endless.*"
—MOTHER TERESA

HERE'S A BIT of personal history on the subject of kindness. I was raised the son of a kind man. I can't even begin to describe the number of times that someone who knew my father has said, "Your dad was the nicest man I have ever known."

The law of attraction was in full force when it brought my dad to my mother, who likewise was a kind woman. She loved my father, but it never showed more than during World War II, before they were married, when Dad was injured in a freak war accident that left him close to death, hospitalized for a year and then returning with 90 percent of his vision gone. From an attorney to a furniture salesman in the flash of a gunshot, my dad stood on his feet and sold furniture for 35 years and never complained . . . never spoke of what could have been.

I'm going to do that for him now.

CHOOSING A LIFE OF KINDNESS

My father could have had success in law; could have made a lot of money; could have taught his son to fish and play ball; could have driven his daughter on her first date; could have driven on the family vacations that he loved. He could have enjoyed movies and TV; could have enjoyed sporting events with wide fields and great views; could have enjoyed watching the sun set.

But he couldn't do any of those things, due to his injury. He also could have complained, moaned, and lived a life of anger and resentment. He could have come home every day and talked about his lousy job and how tired he was after standing on his feet all day. He could have complained about how he was selling the furniture that he had dreamed his family would someday have for the new homes he dreamed he would someday own.

Instead, he chose of life of kindness—a choice *he made*—and he made people feel good to be around him. I still recall, beginning as a young boy and all through adulthood, how I actually felt better when people were around my parents, receiving their kindness and giving it back. How it felt good to see the kind way they treated each other. How I could sense this feeling, and feel better in their presence. To this day, at their gravesides, I still experience this feeling.

As the rest of this chapter will show, I have a reason for sharing this story with you.

WE'RE WIRED FOR KINDNESS

Have you ever done something nice for someone and left "just feeling better"? Of course you have. Did you know that there's a scientific reason for this?

One evening during the course of writing this book, I came across one of my favorite authors, Dr. Wayne Dyer, on a PBS broadcast. I have read many of Dyer's books and find him to be of a spiritual nature that I both admire and follow. To my surprise, Dyer discussed the subject of kindness (remember . . . no coincidences). What he said was interesting and new to me.

There is a brain chemical in our body called *serotonin*. Serotonin is described as a neurotransmitter that has many effects, one of which is to simply make you feel good. Doctors prescribe it to patients suffering from clinical depression. It is also proven to be an aid to our immune system. In short, it is good for us.

Here is what was so interesting in what Dyer said (which I was able to verify). It has been clinically proven that when a person performs an act of kindness, additional serotonin is released into the body, thus making the person feel better. It also has been proven that these levels are increased when we receive—or even simply witness—acts of kindness.

It now became clear to me why I felt so much better while at the Baddour Center, or talking to the folks at L.L.Bean, or walking into St. Jude or the headquarters of Chick-fil-A, or any of the other companies discussed in this book. It was my release of serotonin. It was the kindness that I felt.

I'm going to submit to you, then, that *the secret to owning your customers is to treat them with kindness in every transaction that takes place.*

This is where the revolution begins. Whatever it is that your customer contact people are doing, have them add kindness to each contact. When it comes to anyone in your organization who has any contact with customers, from receptionist to CEO, from sales rep to administrative assistant, from waitress to attendant, make sure that whatever they are serving is served with kindness. All employees must practice this with all customers. There are no exceptions to this rule. None. Angry customers, nontipping customers, any size, shape, or age—if you want them back, treat them with kindness.

Kindness attracts customers. People prefer to do business with people who are nice to them. However, kindness does not come naturally to all people. Some people have difficulty showing regard for others. You must remember that showing kindness in business assists in attracting the type of employees and customers you want.

Let me clarify something for you here. Many people who desire leadership roles confuse kindness with passivity or lack of leadership ability. Nothing could be further from the truth. Kindness should not be confused with timidity. I am not advocating passivity, nor do I have any problems with being assertive when it is necessary. I am saying, however, that if it makes us feel better and make us healthier, why in the world would we not all be kind to each other?

HOW LARGE IS YOUR BLIND SPOT?

During my customer service seminars, I introduce my attendees to the concept of the *blind spot*. The blind spot involves the concept that each of us has behavior we display that we are not aware of, behavior that causes us to be seen differently from the way we desire. This usually comes as a result of taking a behavioral strength to an extreme, such as being so decisive as to appear domineering, or being so analytical as to appear nit-picking. Few people want to appear to be jerks, but many come across just that way, thanks to their blind spots.

I have a business associate I know well enough to know that he is a nice man. He is a dedicated father and successful in his business. However, he gets so focused on business that he forgets to show kindness and regard for others. He reflects indifference. He gets short and impatient when others affect his business progress. He has a large blind spot. He thinks he is being seen as decisive, strong, and powerful. Others often see him as impatient, domineering, and unkind. Many people who come into contact with him do not like his company and avoid him. He does not realize how often he is seen like this, and he would not be pleased to be made aware of the way that so many others view him.

One interesting aspect of human behavior involves observing

people who do not display traits of kindness. They tend to be abrasive, impatient, and even rude. They don't listen—they don't show interest in others, and they show indifference in their communication. In short, they are simply not very nice! What you will find, however, is that these same people still prefer to be around people who are kind. They want to be listened to, they want respect, and they want to be shown regard.

THE LAW OF ATTRACTION AND CUSTOMER SERVICE

Science has proven that everything is energy. Everything. The law of attraction involves the understanding of energy and the role it plays in our lives. Energy is what we are . . . we are not made of energy, we *are* energy. This is fact, not theory. There is no room for misunderstanding this; physicists have shown this for years.

When we begin to understand this more clearly, we can better determine how things around us happen. The understanding that energy attracts similar energy explains everything from how we can be thinking of someone and then that person calls us to how we can continuously become that which we constantly think about.

It can also explain how some companies attract kind people.

Suspend your skepticism and disbelief for a moment, and accept the theory of the law of attraction. Accept the fact that energy attracts like energy. Since we are energy ourselves, we will conclude that we will attract "us." Upbeat "us" will attract other upbeat people. Likewise, negative "us" will attract negative people. Take a moment and reflect on your moods and actions over the course of time and see this for yourself. Did you ever have someone on your mind, and then he or she called you, or you ran into that person mysteriously? This is not a coincidence, but the law of attraction. Thoughts are energy, and what you think, you will attract. It works all the time.

What you think of, you will attract. The law of attraction makes that promise. Think success, and you will succeed. Think of the reasons why you will fail, and you will fail. The same is true for virtually any endeavor you decide to undertake. You can actually attract your result.

YOU CAN ATTRACT THE CUSTOMERS YOU WANT

Your actual energy level is going to attract employees with comparable energy levels. The energy levels I am referring to here easily can be termed *values*. These values are manifested as energy, and the energy that you put out will attract like energy. For example, dignity will attract dignity; respect will attract respect. Greed will likewise attract greed; distrust will attract distrust. In this way, your energy, your values, will attract a certain kind of employee.

Now, take the law of attraction one level further, and extend it to the sales and customer contact people you have recruited. Their energy is going to have the same attraction effect on prospects and customers. The ones who will be drawn to them will tend to share their values. The results are amazing, predictable, and controllable.

Once you understand the law of attraction, you can see why some companies attract different customers than others—customers who are more cheerful, more patient, more loyal. They are attracted to that type of employee. Ditto for customers with less patience, less loyalty, more anger. They find their way to companies represented by that type of employee.

Look for yourself. Observe what kind of customers deal with certain companies. You'll find loyal customers who have an appreciation for the values of certain companies. Chick-fil-A has a different customer base from the typical fast-food restaurant. The Chick-fil-A values will attract a certain client. Nordstrom has a different customer base from most retail stores. The company's values will attract a certain shopper. Look within your industry and see who is loyal to whom. Then look at the employees within those companies.

THE ONION EFFECT

Recent comments by deposed Enron leader Ken Lay that he didn't know what his underlings were doing shouldn't come as a surprise to anyone familiar with the law of attraction. The leaders of Enron, Tyco, WorldCom, and every other company, for that matter, are going to attract others in their organization with values similar to their own. I think you can prove this with what I call the *onion effect*. Peel back the layers of a company, and at the center is the core . . . the values of the company. More specifically, the core of the company consists of the values of the senior executives.

If the core values are of trust, honesty, kindness, diversity, dignity, and respect, then this group will attract other leaders with those same values. They will transcend those values to the treatment of employees, who will likewise transfer those same values to customers. Similarly, companies whose leaders' values consist of distrust, dishonesty, hate, prejudice, indignity, and disrespect will attract management with similar values, which will then find their way to customers via the employees they attract. Simple but true.

Ken Lay claims that he didn't know what Andrew Fastow was doing. I believe him. He didn't have to. He attracted a certain value-driven behavior of his subordinates by *his own* behavior. His manager acted like Ken Lay would have acted.

I have observed the onion effect in many companies and find

it to be intriguing and unfailing. Basically, every layer of a company is a reflection of the previous layer's value system. Beginning at the core, the central base of the organization starts to recruit. The law of attraction assures that they will attract similarly valued people to the organization. As the numbers of people grow, support systems are put into place. This is where the onion effect actually begins.

Systems are implemented that again reflect the values of the principals and leaders of the company. The difference in values is reflected in observing details such as personnel benefits, costs spent on acquiring new customers (rather than on serving existing customers), and similar assessments. Basically, tracking where money is spent at the corporate level creates a clear view of the values of the corporation. As the corporation grows, there are more and more layers. The layers become another reflection of the last until the customer contact layer. This can be people, systems, or both. In either instance, they again reflect the values that go all the way back to the center, to the core. In every example of the companies I have studied, I have never found this to be an incorrect barometer of the values of the company.

Notice the actions of other leaders in business and politics. Watch how their "lieutenants" behave. You'll again see the law of attraction at work. I am not referring to the simple acts of following corporate policy or law. We can all follow something that is clear and spelled out. I am referring to decisions made that involve values, doing the right thing as opposed to the wrong thing.

Want to know how to determine how *your* company will respond under pressure? What kind of management you will be attracting? What kind of customer will want to do business with you? Easy. Gather your executives right now, and find out what it is that is most important to them. Is it family, honor, or dignity? Or is it personal financial success, ego, or power? Although many of you may be disappointed, this is a snapshot of your company's values. And just like a snapshot of the family reunion, companies are nothing more than a reflection of the values that the individuals represent. These values are passed down from one to another.

Take a look around, and validate for yourself. From political administrations to the businesses you read about in the local paper, the values are obvious and predictable. The results are as well.

EMPLOYEES WITH VALUES ARE SELF-POLICING

One of my best friends is a very successful high-school basketball coach here in Memphis. He may even be the best in Memphis history, winning five state championships during his career. His teams have been nationally ranked for four years in a row by *USA Today*. He teaches values, teamwork, respect, and fair play to his players. He is well respected by his players' parents, his peers, and the community. His players reflect his values, and they play like he coaches . . . with respect and dedication to their craft. They play hard, play clean, and win.

There is another high-school coach here in town whose team plays my friend's team every year. His players are always more athletic and always bigger. They are loud, tough, and known for hard-hitting and somewhat dirty play. They consistently beat most everybody in town . . . except one team. They go to the state tournament and never win. My friend's team does.

The other coach's team reflects the values of the coach. He is loud and crude, and he has been disciplined for inappropriate behavior both on and off the court. He does not command much respect, and, accordingly, neither do his players.

What I find interesting about this situation is that, in asking my friend about his players, he explained that they attract players who are like them. They actually "police" themselves and mold the younger players into the type of players they are. When asked whether they would accept thugs and dirty players, my friend quickly said, "No way; they won't stand for that."

The coach's values attract a certain type of player, and the players' values attract like players. The same is true in business. The leader's values attract a certain type of leader; their values attract a certain type of employee. Those employees then attract a certain type of customer.

Peel back the layers of the onion, get to the core, and watch the law of attraction work. You'll be amazed.

KINDNESS ATTRACTS KINDNESS

Assuming that we accept the fact that kindness makes us feel better, why is it that more of us don't practice this in our daily interaction with customers and coworkers? I think that there are numerous answers to this question.

For one thing, many of us look at business as a "war" or "battle." We do our business in a manner that emphasizes speed and efficiency, almost at the expense of everything else. Quick and profitable become the priorities over slower and kinder. And why not? Aren't efficiency and bottom line what are being taught in school? I don't remember being offered one course on kindness during college.

I recently had dinner meetings with two different colleagues. The first one is a nice guy, but not too focused on being kind. He likes "efficient." When the waiter came over, my client didn't make eye contact with him, didn't listen to the specials, and pretty much ignored the efforts of the waiter. Our service was good, but that was it.

Two nights later, I went to the same restaurant with another client. This client was more open, kinder. He stopped talking as the waiter (the same one as earlier) described the specials. He called the waiter by name and thanked him each time he poured water or brought a drink. Our service was exceptional, and the evening was delightful. I am thoroughly convinced that the kindness of the second evening was simply reciprocated and that it led to a better overall experience.

I am continually confused as to why certain people are not kinder when they are either serving or being served. Why don't more people treat their customers or service providers with a little more consideration than they do?

With this quest in mind, I began to ask just that question of certain friends, colleagues, and clients: Why aren't people more polite in their dealings?

The first person I asked was an executive in customer advocacy with a major software company. "I don't think people realize the impact they have on others when they are kind," she said. "I don't think they understand that it goes from table to table, or from customer to customer."

I also asked an executive who has much experience in dealing with call centers, the core of customer service providers. Here is what he said: "Generally speaking, it is the result of stress on the service side. Customer service reps are so stressed that they can't convey kindness to their core of customers. They are worked so hard and are under so much pressure to take calls, they become stressed, and it shows."

"Too busy" was another common response among the business leaders I asked. "Too busy" to be kind to each other. I would submit that this is a sad commentary on the state of business today.

HOW MUCH TIME DOES KINDNESS TAKE?

Are we actually too busy to be kind to each other when doing business? Will it slow us down to take some time to be kind? I guess it might be appropriate to define just what I mean by "being kind." Those words apparently mean different things to different people.

In the examples of the companies I discussed earlier, the word that best describes an attitude of kindness that I found was "empathy." Each of the companies that I interviewed placed tremendous value on understanding the situations of their customers—from being in a rush to get a chicken biscuit at Chick-fil-A to bringing a child in for treatment at St. Jude—and on responding in an understanding way. Does it take more time? Possibly. Does it take more work? Definitely. Does it create a memorable experience? Absolutely.

These companies don't confuse empathy with sympathy. Sympathy is feeling sorry for the situation of the other person. Empathy is actually understanding the feelings of the other person. There's a big difference.

You might ask, "How can someone claim to understand how a parent of a cancer-stricken child feels unless they have had a child with that same problem?" Good question. You can't. But you *can* understand feelings of fear, concern for your child, confusion, denial. You *can* understand that one might act differently when faced with those feelings. And you *can* take those feelings into consideration when dealing with that parent. That is empathy. That is kindness.

So, if you have ever experienced *feelings*, not necessarily exact situations, you are prepared to empathize with the feelings of the person with whom you are dealing. It is that simple. Have you ever been frustrated? Then you know how it feels. Have you ever been angry? Then you know how it feels. Ditto with scared, impatient, fearful, confused, sad, and on and on. Your experience with feelings qualifies you to show empathy with others.

Showing empathy leads to kindness. Look at it this way: Have you ever said to yourself, "If this person knew what I was feeling right now, they would treat me differently"? Of course you have. "If this person knew that I had a sick child waiting for this medicine, they'd fill the prescription quicker." "If this person knew that my car was running, they'd check me out faster." "If this person knew that I had just gotten bad news from work, they'd understand my being a little rude." And if this sounds to you like customers are saying, "Me, me, me," it is because they are, they are, they are!

I sometimes wonder whether people think they buy the right to be rude when they purchase a product or service. In other words, does *the customer* have the privilege to be discourteous when being served? That's kind of a mixed-up way of looking at things.

However, customers don't get paid to be nice, but we do. It would be *easier* if they were nice, but we as service providers are getting paid for this, so suck it up and learn the rule. If you want to own your customers, treat them with kindness.

KINDNESS STARTS AT THE TOP

When I speak to groups of business executives, I can sense an uneasy feeling in some areas of the room or auditorium when I state the following: "You CEOs and senior managers should not be surprised when you hear that your employees are treating your customers with indifference if *you* are treating your employees with indifference."

Simply stated, most employees will treat your customers the way they are treated themselves. Treat your employees with dignity and respect; expect them to treat your customers the same way. Treat your employees with indifference; watch the same with your customers.

The best companies I discovered during my quest were successful in creating a culture of kindness within itself, which filtered its way down throughout the firm. These companies, without exception, were either founded upon, or are currently being led by, principles that are measurable and clearly communicated throughout the organization.

Here is a litmus test for any company: Observe the behavior of the senior management. Do they show compassion? Kindness? Dignity? Courtesy? If so, be assured that they will attract employees of that same kind and that a culture of service will grow. These companies will prosper and do well.

However, find me a company whose leadership is nonempathic, insensitive, and unkind. You can bet that they will attract similar management and employees. And this will be the culture that will carry over to their customers. I want to compete with these companies because they don't own their customers.

SHOW KINDNESS BY "LEARNING" YOUR CUSTOMERS

A friend of mine recently gave me a column authored by Harvey Mackay. Mackay is the chairman of Mackay Envelope Corporation, but he also is well known for his book *Swim with the Sharks without Being Eaten Alive* (New York: Random House, 1988). In that column ("Humanize Your Selling Strategy," *Harvard Business Review*, March–April 1988), Mackay discusses the importance of learning the favorites and preferences of your customers and then using them to make your customers feel special. This entails everything from remembering birthdays and anniversaries to sending holiday gifts that have special meaning based upon the customers' hobbies and habits. In the column, Mackay writes, "The best salespeople are 'other conscious.' They don't do things to people; they do things for people after they have learned something about those people."

I found this to be compelling . . . and true. This caused me to think about some of the companies with which I do business and how little they know about me. It also caused me to think about how little effort it would take for them to get to know me a little and how much it would mean to me if they did.

Let me give you an example. I have a favorite restaurant. I know the manager there, and he is gracious any time I go in. It is an upscale restaurant; dinner and drinks for two will run me over $100. I will go there at least once a month, and I always take my boys there for their birthdays and for Christmas, running into tabs of over $500 for the groups we have. Annually, I will spend well over $5,000 at this restaurant.

This restaurant owns me. The staff are universally polite and professional, and they provide fine service, but more important, they make my party feel special whenever we visit. This is the first place I want to eat when I go out.

The important thing to note about this relationship is that it began prior to my being such a regular customer. The frequency of my business came as a result of their service, not the other way around. They did not notice my being a regular and then commit to service; they committed to service, and that led to my being a regular guest.

Most of the companies that I do business with tend to "know" me about the time they think I am going to buy something from them. My cable company really starts to "know" me when I want to upgrade my service. My insurance company gets really "knowing" when I need some additional coverage. A computer dealer almost has a band play when I walk in to look at the new models. They "know" me then! But the rest of the time, they don't. So, none of these businesses owns me—they rent me until the company that really knows me comes along.

One of my favorite commercials today is the one in which a person is mistaken for a parent at a function, such as a wedding, and turns out to be the financial planner. The planner was so close to his customer that he was mistaken as family. The reason this ad is funny is because it is so foreign to what we as customers and clients are used to.

THE *CHEERS* MODEL OF CUSTOMER SERVICE

One of my recent radio guests was Michael Synk, who is a professional speaker and customer service advocate. Michael has developed a model based on the different kinds of customers who frequented the bar in the TV sitcom *Cheers.* According to Synk, the best customer in the group of characters was Norm, who was in the bar on a regular basis and probably spent more money there than anyone else. Some of the other customers included Cliff, who was there often but didn't spend as much money; Frasier, who stopped in a lot but often left without much more than a cup of coffee; and Lilith, who frequented the place and actually caused other customers to leave. The analogies used by Synk in his model can be effective for any company in its customer service efforts. Obviously, the quest is for more Norms and fewer Liliths.

During an interview on my show, Mike said that companies should actually do an inventory of their customers from time to time and determine which ones they want to keep. I was somewhat surprised to hear what Mike was saying. He repeated that there are customers who should be "fired" by their service providers. These are customers who are actually not benefiting the company serving them, customers who are bringing nothing good to the business and, in many aspects, costing the company money. On *Cheers,* Lilith never spent much money in the bar, but her loud, obnoxious presence caused many of the bar patrons to actually get up and leave. She needed to be fired.

I have subsequently asked many owners and executives of companies what they thought of this concept of getting rid of their "bad" customers. I found a large number who admitted that they had never thought of this idea, and virtually the same number who agreed that it made sense to practice.

START A KINDNESS REVOLUTION IN YOUR COMPANY

Tom Peters, in his book *A Search for Excellence* (New York: Warner Books, 1982), states perhaps the most compelling customer service statement I have ever read. I use this often when I speak, and I want to share it with you. It goes like this:

> Commit yourself to performing one new ten-minute act of exceptional customer service every day. Induce your colleagues to do the same. In the course of a year, in a hundred person organization, this will result in 24,000 new acts of kindness and such is the stuff of revolutions.

Maybe it is time that we became revolutionaries on our jobs. There are ways to do this, and they are simple. They probably will not cause you to change one procedure that you currently have in place. They don't require any changes in the main way you do business, only a subtle change of attitude. When put into practice, however, they may result in the most business-affecting decisions you have ever made.

There are steps that any company can take to eliminate indifference and to introduce kindness in its place. When kindness replaces indifference in companies, tremendous results follow.

How would it be to work for a company that adhered to the following values?

- Customer satisfaction is important and emphasized.

- Each employee understands the mission of the organization and his or her role in that mission.

- The emphasis is on people and how to attract the customers and employees we want.

- Employees are empowered to do the right thing.

- Employees have fun while trying to be the best.

- Customer service is at the top of the mind of each employee in the company.

This is the type of company that each owner wants to run, where each employee wants to work, and where each customer wants to do business. These values come directly from the companies we have reviewed in this book. By taking the best of the best, we can learn specific ways to eliminate indifference in the workplace. Each of these values is reviewed as to how they are implemented in the companies reviewed and how they can be introduced into any company, beginning with being valued at the executive level.

These are the steps toward beginning a kindness revolution. Changing techniques and processes at the customer contact level is not enough to change cultures in organizations, which is a critical step toward "owning" customers and toward changing employee attitudes about customers. Rather, the executives must embrace and accept values if a kindness revolution is truly to take place. Otherwise, fixes will be temporary and isolated.

GETTING STARTED

Learn to celebrate the differences among your employees and customers. This is key but overlooked in many companies. It *must* start at the top and flow throughout the company. The process is simple, powerful, and not practiced enough.

The first step involves checking small thinking at the door. Management begins to celebrate the strength of diversity among its employees. Age, gender, race, culture—each begins to be viewed as an asset, not a liability. Values and attitude become the judgment criteria. Acceptance becomes the norm; indifference becomes the exception.

I have known companies that have recognized division within themselves and that have made decisions to "fix" this by implementing company social events to bring the employees together. I also have seen how often this doesn't work. No one wants to be force-fed another event, in the name of team building, that is going to require even more time away from home and family to satisfy the urge of a manger who senses that cracks are developing in the foundation. We've all seen the "This-time-I-really-mean-it—let's-build-a-team" exercise, which results in more wheels falling off later.

YOU CAN'T FAKE IT

If the leaders at the core of a company do not believe in the celebration of the differences among their employees, it can't be faked. Values show through and are detectable. I recently declined the opportunity to speak to some employees at a chain of stores for a pretty nice fee. The company had participated in a survey of its customers (always recommended) and found that its customers were unhappy with the indifference they received at the stores. The call came to me to provide a quick fix in the form of three-hour seminars with the employees. "We need to do something about this now" was the request from the district manager.

This is not an unusual request, but it is an impossible one. Changes in culture are not going to come as a result of a three-hour seminar. The seminar can be a helpful catalyst for change, but changes in culture will come only as a result of consistent practice of certain methods and the ongoing expression of core values.

As I explained my theories in this regard, it became clear that the employees expressed indifference to their customers as a result of the obvious indifference that the employees felt from the executive. His comments were disrespectful to groups under his supervision and certainly should not have been made to a stranger. Realizing that there was nothing I could do for this organization, I declined the assignment.

Human behavior teaches that we tend to hire people who behave like we do and who are like us in a lot of ways. (This can include age, gender, race, and culture.) It is human nature in many instances and understandable in just as many. It is also the kiss of death for companies that wish to grow. You'll find a lot of "good-old boy" (or girl) companies that start out, often successfully, with a "fraternity"-type environment of a cluster of clones. Successful, long-term growth for these companies, however, is going to require that they expand their acceptance of employees to a broader recruiting base to attract the very best that their market has to offer. The companies that "get it" celebrate the differences among their employees and reflect this from the top. It is not force-fed; it comes naturally.

SHOWING RESPECT TO EMPLOYEES

One constant among the companies that get it when it comes to service is the respect they show their employees. It is reflected in their policies, their diversity, and their understanding of the needs of the families that make up their companies. They are indeed extensions of a family with a corporate name.

That said, it amazes me to observe constantly the poor treatment that many companies give to their employees. This poor treatment comes in many forms, but it can be as significant as the corporate benefits and as small as acknowledging employees as they are passed in the hall. It is indifference—the killer attribute.

I recently had lunch with the CEO of one my client companies. This is a very sharp man and one who is interested in his customers and how he can serve them better. However, he is also extremely focused on whatever task is at hand and sometimes pays so much attention to that task that he ignores whatever is going on around him, including the people.

As we ate in his conference room, I noticed that I was having more dialogue with the assistant who was bringing in our lunch. I provided the "thank-yous" and eye contact with the server, while the CEO talked on about service issues. He wanted me to make some candid assessments about the status of his company and abut the customer service attitudes of his employees.

I suggested that he pay extremely close attention to the very small communication signals that the senior management of his firm sent to employees. "You probably don't have an idea of how much very small signals mean to employees, especially new ones and those who take their jobs seriously. Small signals say a lot."

I also suggested that he observe things such as compliments for small tasks, like the lunch that day, and remembering special events of employees, such as births, marriages of children, and others. Acknowledging the things that are important to employees regularly would result in increased employee loyalty and interest, which translates into more care for customers. It always works.

As difficult as it can be, management must ensure that all employees feel equal in the sight of management and executives. This can be especially difficult in smaller companies, but it is important nonetheless. Cliques and appearances of favoritism must be eliminated at any cost. All employees must feel important to an organization if they are going to make customers feel important. The way your employees are treated is going to be the way they treat your customers.

I recently interviewed the CEO of a successful Atlanta-based company on my show. She is a proponent of compassionate customer service and runs a company that is known for its integrity. I asked her whether she felt that her employees paid attention to her actions around the office. "Definitely," she responded. "I am aware of every movement I make because they watch intently. It is not a feeling of scrutiny, but more an awareness that they want to emulate my actions. I am proud of that feeling and take it very seriously."

I went on to tell this executive that during the process of scheduling the radio interview, I had called her office and received a special feeling of importance from her receptionist. I felt as if my call was important, and it made me feel special. It reminded me that customers don't remember what we say but rather how we say it. I knew that this communication from the receptionist reflected the values of the CEO, and it was apparent during the interview that this was how she felt.

MAKE EACH EMPLOYEE FEEL OWNERSHIP

People take better care of what they own. Whether it is cars, homes, or games, time shows that ownership leads to more care than renting or borrowing does. The same is true in business. Your employees will take better care of your business if they feel a sense of ownership.

This can be promoted in a number of ways. Some companies actually allow employees to purchase equity in the company. I like it when I see business owners give opportunities for equity participation in companies. I think that employees feel a special pride in literal ownership of the companies for which they work.

This is not feasible in all companies, however, especially smaller ones that might have numerous investors who would have difficulty with diluting their investments or with other related situations. Many similar instances make employee ownership difficult.

There is nothing, however, preventing employee ownership in business processes. You'll find that employees will take a special pride of ownership of business practices if they are given an opportunity to participate in the process. It is surprising to me how rarely companies take advantage of the knowledge of their frontline employees to help in improving the process of serving their customers.

DON'T COMPROMISE—DO THE RIGHT THING

I'm now going to give you a bonus case study—another company to be emulated, whose founder instilled values practiced after he was gone. When I asked around about customer service in fast food, I kept getting sent to Chick-fil-A. When I asked about values in companies of all types, however, the name Dave Thomas, the founder of Wendy's, kept coming up. Prior to his death in 2000, Thomas ran Wendy's based upon five values, which are known and practiced by all of Wendy's employees. They are:

> #1. *Quality is our recipe.* Thomas believed that the quality of the food served at Wendy's was the foundation of its success. Each franchise was expected to maintain that quality to the highest degree, so that customers would always know exactly what to expect when they ate at a Wendy's.
>
> #2. *Do the right thing.* Thomas was known for being a man of his word and expected it from Wendy's employees. He also taught the practice of "empowering" his employees with

enough authority to make decisions on integrity at the expense of profits.

#3. Treat people with respect. Thomas also believed that respect was another important ingredient in Wendy's success. He felt that the best way to show respect is by using people's names. Wendy's employees are still taught to learn—and to use—customers' names whenever possible.

#4. Profit is not a dirty word. Thomas felt that when customers were taken care of, the bottom line took care of itself. He also believed, however, that businesses exist to make money.

#5. Give something back. Wendy's employees are encouraged and supported to give back to their respective communities.

Dave Thomas was one of the most admired men in America, and the respect that he enjoyed runs deep today among Wendy's employees. This respect is based upon his beliefs in the values described above and his unwavering support of them. The annual report for Wendy's still refers to Thomas's values and his commitment to "do the right thing." As a matter of fact, Thomas was known for using a three-point checklist to determine whether, on *every* action that an employee is empowered to make, he or she is doing the right thing.

Thomas's list is used by the cadets at West Point when there is a question as to whether something is honorable. These are the three key questions:

1. Does this action attempt to deceive anyone or allow anyone else to be deceived?

2. Does this action gain, or allow the gain of, a privilege or advantage to which I or someone else would not otherwise be entitled?

3. Would I be satisfied with the outcome if I were on the receiving end of this action?

DON'T FIGHT—MAKE IT RIGHT

Here's a story that demonstrates another business owner's commitment to providing the best customer service he could—no questions asked. Only this doesn't involve a well-known name or a large national company. This is simply someone who "gets it" when it comes to customer service.

A few years ago, I got a call from my next-door neighbors. It was around Thanksgiving, and this couple, being good friends of mine, were not reluctant to call me for help.

Pat had purchased an artificial Christmas tree from a florist in town during a summer special. It was an elaborately lit tree that required assembly. It was gorgeous and large. It was not easy to assemble, but it was indeed going to be beautiful when it was put together.

Pat had gotten a nice discount and looked forward to the season when the tree would be in place. Michael, her husband, was assembling the tree and found a section that wouldn't light up. After some frustration, they called me to ask whether I could help.

We worked collectively with no success on getting the section of the tree to light up. After an hour or so, we gave up. It was around 8:00 or 8:30 in the evening, and we were tired of the whole experience. The tree was not going to work without the lights, so I told Pat to find her receipt and to call Frank Gray Florist the next day. Pat explained that the receipt was nowhere to be found and that she didn't have any type of proof of purchase, warranty, or any other record of where she had bought the tree. Pat decided that she would call Frank Gray Florist and leave a message to call her back the next day. Michael and I chuckled at the thought of a small company's owner getting a call for an exchange or refund of a purchase made at a substantial discount five months earlier, and with no receipt.

Frank Gray answered the phone that night. It was the busy season, and he was working late. When Pat told him of our dilemma, all he asked was her address. Twenty minutes later, Frank knocked on the door and came in to help. He worked with the tree for a while and determined that it was indeed faulty. "I was afraid of this," he said, "so I brought another one just in case."

With that, he went to his truck and brought in a brand-new tree. He spent the next twenty or thirty minutes helping us put up the beautiful tree. He never asked for a receipt, never asked for "proof of purchase," was extremely gracious, and left with a "Merry Christmas."

LETTING ALL EMPLOYEES KNOW THAT THEIR JOBS ARE IMPORTANT

My youngest son, Wilson, played on a championship football team in high school. He was a lineman. If you follow football, you know that a position on the line is not a glorious one. The linemen don't get much glory; they don't make the headlines. They do their job quietly and without a lot of recognition.

That particular year, the team had an extremely strong line. They also had a talented backfield consisting of a couple of dynamic running backs with exceptional talent. Before the season began, reporters from the local papers began to follow the team, paying particular interest to the running backs. However, something interesting happened that I observed and have used with my business clients.

The running backs would refer to the strength of the line when discussing the upcoming season with the TV and newspaper reporters. They made sure to share the credit. As a result, the linemen were interviewed by the media. They, in turn, bragged about the talented running backs. During the season, the backs excelled and got most of the headlines, but they continued to give credit after each game to the linemen. Pictures of the line appeared in the media; they began to be recognized unlike any others in the area. They were given a nickname; they had an identity. The groups shared the glory; they were undefeated during the season and went to the state championship as a unit.

When people learn that credit will find its place within their organization, they become a team. Credit should be given, not taken. It will always find its rightful place. If an employee does something successful, the best advice I can give is to share the credit with others on the team. While many will feel that this is giving away what they have worked for, the reality is that the credit will find its way to the rightful recipient. The team, however, will feel appreciation for the sharing of the credit and will work even harder over time. This is the essence of the team concept; it is what we can learn from the best.

THE PROCESS OF SERVICE

Anyone who listens to my radio shows or hears me speak knows that my emphasis on customer service is centered on the people aspect rather than on the process. I have friendly debates and get somewhat passionate about the importance of attitude and people when it comes to service. I don't believe that any process works with the wrong people, and believe the right people will make up for a lack of process. That said, the combination of people and process makes for an unbelievable customer experience.

In the next few chapters, I want to focus on what that process should include so that you can make sure that customers are *wowed* each time they do business with your company. I am going to focus now on the "every contact" process, which your employees should practice with every customer they meet.

These basics are not effective if not practiced. They must be at the top of each employee's mind every day, every contact. They are just as described—basics. Your particular company may add some specific basics of its own, but these are to be included in every customer experience to ensure that you are set apart from your competition. They will eliminate the appearance of indifference in your company and, with the right people practicing them, will result in your owning your customers. They are a combination of the finest processes followed by the companies we have discussed, and they should be practiced religiously because of one simple truth: They work.

I am more concerned than ever about the level of service that companies offer today. In a service economy, the United States is losing what edge it has had as a leader in service. I am constantly being told of stories of exceptional service in Europe and Asia and that this is the norm, that this is what's expected abroad. I am told that they currently "get it" better than we do.

As a result, my quest continues. I want to learn from the best, such as those companies discussed in this book, but I also want to continue to explore why the rest of us are no longer getting it, why we are not providing the world standard for service.

CHAPTER ELEVEN

HOW TO ELIMINATE INDIFFERENCE IN YOUR WORKPLACE

"*My religion is very simple. My religion is kindness.*"

—THE DALAI LAMA

THE COMMON ELEMENT among the companies providing the finest customer service is how they use core values to eliminate indifference in their workplace. By emphasizing dignity, respect, courtesy, and kindness, they create a culture of values and make their employees and customers feel important. As a result, a process that they each practice with every customer contact becomes almost automatic.

Some of these companies, such as The Ritz-Carlton, have identified this process and list the steps for employees to remember. Others, such as St. Jude Children's Research Center, haven't gone to the extent of writing the rules down, but they practice them just the same. It is part of the culture of the organization; it is as natural to the employees as breathing. It is part of their value structure.

I am going to attempt to list these basic tenets. They constitute a fundamental process that should be practiced with every customer contact. Keep in mind, too, that your employees will treat your customers the way you treat them, so these basic rules should also be utilized in your communication with your employees.

These are rules of engagement; they are not meant to be simply written down and left on a page. They must be implemented to create a culture of kindness and to eliminate indifference. I am listing them in no particular order, as they each carry their own value. I am purposely not numbering them, so as to emphasize their equal value. There is no significant number associated with these rules, such as "20 Rules" or "15 Secrets" or anything else.

These are simply the methods that I have gleaned from observing how the best service providers do it. I submit to you that practicing these rules will lead to a significant reduction, if not elimination, of indifference in your workplace. Your employees and customers will feel important, and you will own them. Practice them, and see for yourself what a difference they make.

RULES FOR ELIMINATING INDIFFERENCE IN THE WORKPLACE

- *Use your customer's name.* The use of someone's name reflects respect for the other person. If you don't know the name, ask. If not sure about pronunciation, ask. Likewise, give the other person your name when first introduced, whether in person or on the phone. Most of the customer contact reps in the companies discussed in this book wear name tags to make it easier for customers to use names when doing business with them. I strongly recommend this for customer contact reps. There is one other important point to be made here: Make sure to eliminate slang use and "cutesy" names. Eliminate the "honeys," "sweeties," and "sweethearts" that might be floating around the office.

- *Make eye contact.* You show your regard or disregard for another person during the first fifteen seconds that you are with them. That's how long it takes to let another person know whether you think they are important to you or not. This initial regard comes in the form of eye contact. Whether walking down the hall, greeting a shopper, or serving a customer, make eye contact with the other person. The talk about "our customers are important" is nothing more than talk if not practiced with employees. Acknowledge them with eye contact at each meeting. Ask yourself, "Whom would I rather work for—someone who makes me feel important, or someone who doesn't?" Showing regard is the best way to make someone feel important; making eye contact is the best way to show regard.

- *Find out what is important to them.* I have observed that the best companies pay attention to what is important to both their employees and their customers. They focus on what is important to their employees, which leads to their employees focusing on what is important to their customers. I have personally met with an employee who had the special title of "CEO of Fun." Her job included keeping aware of what was going on within the company regarding employees, as well as scheduling regular events around charitable and civic endeavors that included all the employees. She made sure that she knew what was important to the employees and then made sure that it was remembered and celebrated. The company she works for is known for its outstanding service and has experienced fast growth. It also has a reputation as (guess what) a fun place to work.

- *Practice active listening.* Whatever survey, book, or data you look at, you'll find that the single largest complaint about interpersonal communication is poor listening. This is especially true in customer service. Poor listening leads to poor service. Effective listening will lead to better service. The companies that "get it" when it comes to service know the value and importance of listening. Active listening involves letting the person who is speaking know that you are processing what he or she is saying. You can do this with small signals, such as nodding your head as the person speaks and acknowledging what he or she says, with frequent comments such as "Yes" or "I understand." Where appropriate, you should respond directly to what the other person is saying. Active listening shows clearly that the information is important to you and that it is being processed as communicated. It also reinforces the idea that something will be done, since the data are being received clearly.

- *Always say, "Thank you" and "My pleasure."* I admit that this is right off the Ritz-Carlton card, but it is powerful advice for any company. Once the habit of saying both of these phrases is established, they become enormously powerful tools. Acknowledging an act by saying, "Thank you" shows regard; acknowledging a "Thank you" by saying, "My pleasure" shows regard as well. The use of these words might be difficult at first, but once it is part of your company's natural dialogue, it will become natural and much noticed and appreciated by your customers. These seemingly small changes in the way you treat your employees and customers are what lead to the large changes in image.

- *Practice nondefensive behavior.* The companies that get it when it comes to service believe that their customer is always "right." What this means is that these companies do not argue with their customers even when the customer is in error. They don't try to change the customer's mind. They are in business to correct customer problems, and they have come to realize that correcting problems is a better way to change customers' points of view than being defensive or argumentative with their customers. They focus on one thing when there are problems—fixing them. Defensive behavior ruins relationships. The best way to convince someone that your company is good is to *be* good, not to *talk* good. Fix the problem.

- *Pay attention to your telephone etiquette.* When you ask people what frustrates them as customers, you'll repeatedly hear complaints about the telephone communications of companies. I still am amazed at companies that treat their telephone system like it is the back door of their business. There are far too many companies that simply don't realize how poor an image they present when people call them. Telephone courtesy is emphasized at the world-class service providers. (Remember the chapter on L.L.Bean?) Simple nuances such as asking before putting someone on hold, introducing callers on a transfer, and making it easy and quick to speak to someone are what separate the best from the rest. Never forget that the person on the telephone with your customer is your company. Are you proud of the way they represent you? Someone should be checking this out periodically.

- *Celebrate the differences.* Another of the common traits of the best service providers is their acceptance of the fact that there are different ways to approach different problems and customer issues. They recognize that not every employee is going to behave the same way in the same situations, and they urge their employees to use good judgment in making individual decisions when solving problems. Their managers and supervisors don't emphasize "Do it my way" but rather "Do it the right way." As a result, employees feel that they are accepted for their individuality and are not made to feel stereotyped. Their differences are considered assets, not liabilities.

- *Remember that every job is important.* Employees must be made to feel that their job is important and critical to the mission of the company. This should be true of every single job in the firm. If the job is not important, it should be eliminated. Management must take responsibility to let each employee realize that his or her job is important. Practice using recognition, thank-yous, and other ways of simply, but consistently, letting employees know and understand what value their job brings to the company. This makes their efforts more important and helps to keep each team member focused on the greater mission of the company.

- *Use your best judgment, and give others leeway to do the same.* This is one of the most important rules of world-class service. Employees must be given room to err. They must be given opportunity to make decisions and to observe the impact of their decisions on their customers. Similarly, employees must be made to feel that their judgment is supported by management, and that when their judgment is in error, management will work to avoid future repetition of the same error, rather than feeling that they will be punished for their decisions. This process ensures growth of employees and a continual improvement of service. Taking a customer issue "to management" should be virtually eliminated within your company.

- *If you see a problem, fix it.* The "it's not my job" syndrome also must be eliminated from your company. The excuse that a problem is not a particular person's responsibility is just that—an excuse. It is not a legitimate reason to take no action to solve or avoid a problem. Employees should be taught that organizational charts have nothing to do with solving a customer problem. If a customer needs something, get it.

- *Cleanliness reflects care.* This is an important aspect of customer service, and many companies that I observe overlook it. Management should understand that, right or wrong, cleanliness is often associated with quality. Human nature reflects that when something is cared for, it is usually kept clean. The same is reflected in a business. The appearance of cleanliness reflects a care for the business. Customers observe this.

- *If you are in management, you are being observed.* I want you to remember what it was like when you first began your career in business. Do you remember how closely you watched your supervisors and their every move? Every little motion indicated something to you, from their greetings to their eye contact to their body language. Everything said something, and everything was observed. Your managers must understand that they now shoulder this responsibility. They are being watched closely and must be aware of this fact at all times.

- *You are your company.* This one is simple and applies to every employee in the firm. They must remember this rule at all times, and they must be reminded constantly of this rule. Whoever is in contact with a customer *is* the company to that customer. Not your boss, the guarantee, the motto, or the mission statement. The company is you right now.

- *Find out what your customers think.* What the executives in the boardroom think means nothing; what your customers think means everything. Ask your customers what they want, and do it. Ask them what they don't want, and stop doing it.

- *Your employees can make it better.* Your employees are the best way to make your company better. Ask the front desk staff how to improve the front desk operation. Ask the call center agents how to create a better call center. They can tell you how to run a better company. Ask them.

- *Check how you greet your customers.* Take a look at every first contact that a customer can have with your company. Walk in the front door as if you've never walked in before. Call every department that a customer is going to call. Check the look of e-mails that customers get. Take a look as if you are a customer looking at your company for the first time. Make that impression count.

- *To get great customer service, be a great customer.* Don't forget the universal law of attraction. Energy attracts like energy; what you project will be what you will receive. Want to receive kindness? Try generating some kindness. Want respect? Try giving some to your service rep. Watch what you will receive; you'll be surprised.

CHAPTER TWELVE

THE QUICK FIX WON'T WORK

How to Ensure Permanent Change

"*Man who think something is impossible should not stand in way of Man doing it.*"

—CHINESE PROVERB

I OFTEN GET CALLS from companies that have heard my show or read something I have written about customer service. Usually, something has prompted these calls, such as the loss of an important customer or the result of a survey that has not been very good. The callers will request that I go in and do a program for their customer service reps to help them get straightened out. They are looking for a quick fix or magic elixir that can be shared with their employees and that will correct what is wrong and make everything alright with their customers. They don't mind paying a nice fee for that fix. The bad news is this: This kind of quick fix won't work.

Books, tapes, CDs, seminars, newsletters, and speeches abound on the topic of service. Information is everywhere. Customer service is discussed regularly and passionately. In my experience as a radio talk show host, I can vouch for the fact that people want to talk about their service experiences, both good and bad. While they might not talk about "no problem" service, they love to talk about problems—unsolved problems as well as solved problems.

Given this continued interest in customer service, I have wondered why customer service is in the malaise it is today. As a result of the quest I undertook to complete this book, I have begun to understand at least part of the reason why.

I have heard speculation as to the reasons why customer service is at the low level it is today. These reasons are numerous, and a few have been covered in this book. More sophisticated customers, a generational change of employee attitudes toward work, more outsourcing of customer service call centers overseas, and too much technology are frequently mentioned as reasons for the demise of service levels. While I agree that each of these things contributes to the current levels, I don't think any of them is the significant problem. I think the problem goes back to the story at the top of this chapter. Too many companies think there is a quick fix for their customer service problems, as opposed to making a long-term commitment to quality that is accepted by everyone in the organization, top to bottom.

EIGHT TIPS FOR CHANGING YOUR SERVICE CULTURE

If we accept that fact that the quick-fix solutions will not work, what methods of implementing change can be utilized that will indeed result in cultural changes in a company? What are some of the things an organization can do to cause a lasting change in its customer service performance?

1. *Have real expectations of the results of seminars and speakers.* These programs should be used to introduce new ideas or to support existing programs, but never

to be used in lieu of other processes. There is no magic potion for service. It has to be ongoing and an inherent part of the culture of the organization. Seminars and speakers are effective catalysts of service culture, but they are never to be confused with the solution. The solution is the relentless pursuit of service combined with values.

2. *Make sure the top-line executives of the organization know that customer service is serious business to the company.* It cannot be lip service; senior management must take service very seriously. Remember that employees observe management and how it supports this culture. They will act accordingly.

3. *Keep the key issues of the company service beliefs and principles alive via regular meetings and discussions.* The basic service principles of the organization should be mentioned at every meeting in the organization. There should be no exceptions to this. Discussions of the quest for service should be second-nature when meetings occur. Employees should be sincerely commended when they report that they have done something for a customer.

4. *Make sure that written correspondence—from internal memos to e-mail correspondence—includes references to service.* I have a client who has every employee in his firm include one of the company's service basics on the signature line of their e-mails. Every e-mail that they send therefore makes a stated commitment to service. This creates an atmosphere of "lifting the bar" that causes the employees to be consistently

aware that they have stated the importance of service and they must live up to their commitment.

5. *Emphasize the beliefs and principles with new employees.* New employees should have no question regarding the importance of service in the organization. The focus on customer service should be reinforced during any orientation as well as the natural mentoring that will take place with new hires. From interviews, to welcome sessions, to training, through indoctrination, service must be stressed.

6. *Make sure that your company website communicates the passion for service that exists in the organization.* Websites are more and more becoming the front door for businesses. Take a look at the websites of the companies examined in this book, and you'll sense the importance of customer service that is similar to the experience of walking in the front door of the business itself. A website is an extension of the company to prospects and customers in the same way that the receptionist or operator is the front door to your company.

7. *Make sure that executives and managers are interacting with customers.* This is something that I rarely see practiced by any companies. Senior managers too often operate with the concept that they have "paid their dues" and that they don't need to interact with customers any more. They feel they have reached a level that is above spending time with customers and would rather dictate to others in the organization what their customers are thinking and how to deal with them!

8. *Treat your customer service reps as importantly as you treat your sales reps.* If you've ever noticed the lavish awards, banquets, and recognition that most companies heap on their sales representatives, you've probably also noticed the absence of recognition of the customer service contact people. Companies have migrated toward a fairly common belief that the name of the business game is new sales while often losing sight of the fact that it takes more cost to acquire a new customer than it does to maintain an existing one.

CHAPTER THIRTEEN

ARE YOU READY?

"*The secret of getting ahead is getting started.*"
—MARK TWAIN

YOUR COMPANY CAN make a difference in your industry and community as a result of the service you offer. The companies that I write about in this book have all shown this, and it has been validated time and time again. That decision, however, is up to you to make.

This difference does not come as a result of seminars, motivational speakers, memos, annual meetings or reports, or temporary campaigns. If it is not permanent, do not waste your money or time on any of these things. The change has to come from one customer contact after another—one customer at a time, hundreds of times a day, seven days a week; change comes customer by customer.

I would like to issue some final challenges to you readers. If this book has served its purpose as a catalyst for change in your company, I want to ask these questions for you to answer honestly about your company.

1. *Are you ready to guarantee your product or service to every customer you do business with?* Are you willing to tell your customers—all of them—that you proudly stand behind your prod-

uct or service? If they are not happy, will you gladly (with no questions, proof of purchase, evidence of defects, or any other requirements) return their money? Are you willing to tell your employees to do the same if a customer is not happy?

L.L.Bean is.

2. *Are you ready to talk about customer service every day?* Are you willing to have every employee in your organization take a few minutes every day to talk about customer service? Will you provide a few basic points to remember, that will keep service at the top of every employee's mind? Are you willing to take *your* time every day to participate in these meetings? Are you willing to visibly show to your employees that customer service is so important that you commit to participating in long-term programs instead of the latest fad?

The Ritz-Carlton is.

3. *Are you ready to trust your employees to use their best judgment and do the "right thing" without having to check with a manager each time a decision needs to be made?* Are you willing to tell your employees that they were hired because of your confidence in their judgment and values and that you trust them to make decisions in the best interests of both your customers and your company? Are you willing to take the time to find the best people, not the most skilled, and to teach them your industry and the skills needed to achieve success in that industry?

Nordstrom is.

4. *Are you ready to ensure that each employee in your company realizes what they come to work each day to do?* Are you willing to discover the "higher cause" that your company is in business to serve? Are you willing to determine whether you are just cutting stone or building cathedrals? Are you willing to look inside and determine whether the work that you and your employees do serves a purpose or simply serves *your* purpose? Do the employees at your organization know why they come to work each day?

The ones at St. Jude do.

5. *Are you ready to do whatever it takes to make doing business with you an experience that is distinct from dealing with your competitors?* Are you willing to create an environment that makes your customers feel so important that they would be missed if they didn't do business with you? Are you willing to stick to your guns when it comes to maintaining the highest standards for your product and service in the face of early start-up woes and through growth and expansion?

Debbi Fields was.

6. *Are you ready to give up income and wealth because you believe in your values?* Are you willing to look investors in the eye and say, "This is what I believe"—even if it sacrifices business and profits? Are you willing to set an example for your employees to the extent that the benefit might even go to their next employer?

Chick-fil-A is.

7. *Are you ready to make a commitment to a goal, keep that commitment as the focus of your business, and let everyone know how you do in trying to attain that goal, even when you never achieve it?* Are you willing to "put it out there" where each of your employees and customers can see exactly how you are doing?

FedEx is.

8. *Are you willing to make kindness a value that permeates your organization?* Are you ready to take a moment to simply be kind in your dealings with employees and customers alike?

The Baddour Center is.

THE QUEST CONTINUES

Although we are now near the end of this book, it is certainly not the end of my journey. My quest for the best in customer service is ongoing. What I learned from observing and studying the companies chronicled in this book has taught me what to look for in excellence in service.

I often find myself in the discussion of "process versus people" when it comes to customer service. They are both important, but not equally. No process is effective with the wrong people, but the right people will find a way to make things work. In the end, I have found that people are more important than process. The companies that I have presented are by no means perfect. I am not pretending that all of their employees are euphoric in their work or that they have figured out the magic formula for success in business. Each has its own share of internal problems that simply come as a result of doing business. But I did not expect to find perfection when I began my quest. What I did find, however, was a relentless pursuit of goals based upon values. What I found—and now firmly believe—is that a constant focus on values results in a different employee and customer experience. While not perfect, that experience is kind, dignified, and thoughtful. Most important, it is unique and sets companies apart from others.

CHAPTER FOURTEEN

TEN STEPS TO AN EXTREME CORPORATE MAKEOVER

"*If you have always done it that way, it is probably wrong.***"**

—CHARLES KETTERING

THERE'S NOTHING LIKE seeing the concepts you've studied proved in real action. The case study here is based entirely on a client of mine who has experienced in a matter of months a complete corporate culture change by practicing the philosophies of the companies portrayed in this book. I have observed the changes in the company and have seen the powerful differences that these changes have made. This case study is applicable to companies of all types and of most sizes.

The executives of this company have given me permission to tell their story, but I'm not going to use real names. Following the description of their efforts, I'll summarize what was done, how it can be matched step-by-step, and what has been learned from the companies discussed within this book.

LOOKING TO IMPLEMENT CHANGE

The principal owner of this medical software company has owned the company for over ten years. Starting literally from a room in his home, he had grown the company to a small, successful two-million-dollar-plus company. Clients of the company, medical practices, were happy with their service, and business was good, if not robust. After sustaining flat growth for a couple of years, the owner decided to bring in a partner and to attempt to take the company to the next level. His partner is a businessman whom I have known for years through another industry, and he was engaged (now married) to the owner's sister-in-law.

At the time of my first involvement with the company, I had met only the new partner. He and I had known each other through consulting and speaking that I had done with his former company, and we had a pleasant business relationship. I was aware of his involvement with this company and had heard that he was happy with his new situation. One day, I got a call from him, asking whether we could go to lunch.

Over lunch, the new partner asked whether I would help him with a new system that they were planning to install. As part of the efforts to improve their company and to position it for growth, they had decided to improve their client maintenance dispatch process. This included installing a new automated attendant system that would help in routing trouble calls to the correct employee. I was pleased to work with the new partner as I had always enjoyed our work together. But during lunch, it was determined that the principals had taken it upon themselves to implement the change. They had not asked their clients what *they* thought.

We agreed before the end of lunch that it made sense to ask their customers what they thought about not only the proposed changes, but also about the overall service process of the company. The new partner thought this made sense, and wanted to discuss it with both his partner and the staff. (*Note the involvement with both customers and staff here. The opportunity for ownership was offered and accepted and was a good strategic decision.*)

We decided to design and execute a Web-based survey consisting of questions compiled with input from management and staff of the company. *(Note the continued involvement with staff.)* It was during this process that I met the original owner of the company and was quickly able to observe the passion that both owners had in their quest for the best in service. They knew that their product was not their main asset; that was their service and their people. They wanted to learn the best way to use these assets to their customers' advantages. *(Note that they were not hesitant to ask their customers what they thought.)* They were willing to go to all of their customers, not just a selected few, and to ask them what they thought about how the company was doing.

The survey was created, reviewed with staff *(note the staff ownership again)*, and distributed to clients. The results began to come in, and one thing was immediately clear. The planned change for the automated system was not a popular one with this company's clients, so it was scrapped. *(Note how they responded to their clients' wants.)*

The surveys were reviewed, and the results were good. By any standards, they were good. However, they were not good enough for the partners. *(Note the relentless pursuit of excellence. Good enough never is.)*

Based upon some of the answers to the anonymous surveys, the partners decided to create a small focus group of their clients to review and to validate the survey responses as well as introduce the changes that were being planned for the company. *(Note the ownership of change offered to customers here.)* At the focus group meeting, the findings were confirmed via rankings of what was important to the customers as well as affirmations for the new changes. *(Note the appreciation of the customers for being included in the process.)*

As the new trouble-reporting system was being implemented, the partners decided to implement the Ritz-Carlton model of customer service for their company. They had heard my enthusiasm for the model and had seen the card I carry with the Ritz-Carlton credo, motto, and basics on it, and they decided to establish a similar process for their business, something The Ritz-Carlton not only encourages but teaches.

I have had the opportunity to spend time with both the partners of this company as well as company employees. The core concepts of service, respect, humor, and integrity are on display throughout the organization. There is no false pride, no ego. The values at the top permeate throughout the company. The responses of the focus group (which I led and observed) made that clear to me.

Staff meetings are serious when it comes to business, not serious when it comes to the partners. From my perspective, it appears as if people at this company have fun at work. I don't know whether every day is fun. I *do* know that they are on a quest to encourage fun at work. I also know that they achieve it, at least occasionally, as I have seen it personally. *(Note that it is possible for leaders to take their jobs seriously without taking themselves seriously.)*

Using employee input and the Ritz-Carlton model, a credo, a motto, and service basics were suggested and agreed upon. *(Note the use of employee input.)* The credo and motto were put onto virtually every piece of correspondence sent both internally and externally and discussed at every meeting. *(Note the use of "top-of-mind awareness" for keeping the service theme alive.)* Today, regular meetings are conducted at which service levels are reviewed and intense focus is placed on customer improvement.

Surprisingly, this company did not have a website. It also had a fairly basic logo, which did little to reflect the culture or professionalism of the organization. Meetings with web design and marketing experts have created a corporate "makeover" that now reflects the values and service philosophies of the principals.

Now, from e-mails to meetings to the website, there is absolutely no question as to the values and commitment to service that drive this company.

The result is a service-oriented company, led by executives with values and principles that are understood and communicated clearly to the employees of the organization, with a relentless pursuit of excellence. Perfection is not their goal, the quest for excellence is.

I should make one other point here. I had some pretty candid conversations with some of this company's customers around the time of the focus group. They have many customers that won't even think of doing business with their competitors. They have customers that they *own*.

MAKE YOUR COMPANY WHAT YOU WANT IT TO BE

Let's take a look at the step-by-step process that your company can take to make it what you want it to be. By following these steps, in order, you'll see a change in the way your company does business and the way your employees will treat your customers.

Step One: Survey Your Customers

I usually suggest a Web-based anonymous survey with no more than twenty-five questions. The questions should be multiple choice and sent to every customer if possible. If that is not possible, you should attempt to contact a substantial sample of your customer base. Make sure you get input from your employees. Remember what your objective is here. It is to get information from your customers as to ways in which you can improve. We're not suggesting that you play pollster; the objective is information. You can't help but learn more about what your customers are thinking. The best companies are not afraid to find out what their customers are thinking. The mediocre won't touch this.

Step Two: Prepare to Do What Your Customers Want

Asking your customers what they want, and then doing nothing, is a complete waste of time. It does no good at all. When you learn that your customers desire changes, make them! Don't be defensive, and never take the "This is the way we have always done it" stance.

Step Three: Conduct a Small Focus Group to Validate Proposed Changes

When conducting the Web-based survey, ask your customers whether any of them would be willing to participate in a small focus group session. Then, ask them either to contact you or to identify themselves on the survey. Identify a cross-section of your customers and bring them together to share what you learned on the survey, get their comments, and discuss what you intend to do as a result. Your role in these group sessions is to listen and take notes. Often it is prudent to bring in a facilitator for these sessions who can keep the process moving. This will allow company representatives to observe rather than to participate. This can be one of the most effective learning opportunities for companies that want to really know what their customers are thinking.

Step Four: Develop Your Company Credo

This step comes directly from the Ritz-Carlton model of service. It is the first step toward changing the culture in any organization. It is simple but powerful. It involves crystallizing a "statement of service" that becomes the foundation of everything your company does. Without it, it is impossible to know what your company is all about. With it, a culture can be achieved that will permeate throughout the organization to customers. The Ritz-Carlton credo supports its motto, which says it all: "We are Ladies and Gentlemen serving Ladies and Gentlemen." (The complete Ritz-Carlton model can be reviewed on the website at www.ritzcarlton.com under the "Gold Standard" link.) It is imperative that the credo be based upon input from employees to ensure that they take ownership of the fundamental principles and values of the company. The credo expresses the corporate culture of the organization; the motto succinctly summarizes the credo. It should be simple enough to be easily remembered, strategically imprinted so as to be top-of-mind, and so that its importance throughout the organization can be emphasized.

Step Five: Talk About Customer Service Every Day

Once again, The Ritz-Carlton provides a model for the implementation of keeping a service culture alive via its "lineup." Through this brief process every day, each employee reviews the motto, credo, and basics of the organization, as well as what is happening that particular day. There is absolutely no way, over time, that this culture will not be engrained in this manner. It will be impossible for anything else to push it out of the way, but it must be discussed frequently and regularly.

Step Six: Review Customer Objectives Regularly

FedEx sets a good example of the way this works. Its objective is simple. It works for 100 percent success in overnight package delivery. That is its mission, its goal. It doesn't ever make it, but the relentless pursuit of perfection results in success. Each employee can inquire as to how well the company did the night before toward reaching its goal. This is important: keeping employees informed as to the company's success.

Step Seven: Let the Culture Find Its Place

Too many leaders try to "force-feed" cultural changes in their organization, reverting to the "fad of the day" without giving their efforts time to grow. A change in corporate culture will take some time. Some results will be observed quickly, but the complete process will really develop as new people come into the organization. To them, what is happening is not a change; it is what "is." To existing employees, however, this may be viewed as change. Some will resist the change. It is human nature and should be expected. That said, those who resist the change for too long should be weeded out and should be replaced with those who buy into the changing culture. Once the new culture is established, you'll find your company naturally attracting the type of employee you desire. Again, this is a universal law; it will happen.

Step Eight: Put It Out There for People to See

Once your standards are in place, put them out where people can see them. Posters, prints, coffee mugs, whatever; make sure you let your employees and customers know that these standards are important to your company and that you accept the challenge that letting others see them offers. I mentioned one of my clients that has every person in the company have a signature line on their correspondence that includes one of the customer service promises (e.g., "If you see it is broken, fix it."). That way, each communication restates one of the company's principles.

Also make sure that your values, principles, and commitments are clearly stated on your website. This is the front door for prospects, customers, and potential employees. It should be the billboard for what your company believes and what separates you from the rest. I recently watched with interest an interview with an employee of St. Jude at the FedEx St. Jude Children's Research Golf Classic. This is an annual PGA event played in Memphis and benefiting St. Jude. The employee was discussing the importance of the donations the PGA makes and mentioned in passing the work done at St. Jude and used the phrase "saving children's lives." You'll find this reference all over the walls and literature at St. Jude.

Step Nine: Make Your Motto, Credo, Promise, and Basics Part of Your Employees' Uniform

I have observed the impact of having all employees carry some form of note or card, reminding them of what their mission and service commitments are, in their purse or wallet. Bruce Seigel at The Ritz-Carlton carries his in his wallet with his money to be reminded each time he spends money what is behind his ability to *make* money. Others have the information made into desktop reminders. However it is done, your corporate commitments should be "in your employees' faces" all day.

Step Ten: Practice Kindness in Every Transaction, Every Contact

This ingredient will change companies, attract better employees, and attract better customers. But it takes work. Anything other than kindness among employees and customers should not be tolerated. It is free; it costs nothing to bring to your company. It consists of small, barely noticeable actions and has the power to completely revolutionize the culture of the largest company. It has been scientifically proven that kindness makes people feel better and that it is good for their immune systems. It makes them healthier.

THIS WILL WORK IN YOUR COMPANY

I have observed this technique working in companies that have committed to implementing it. When the leaders of an organization accept it, it has dramatic impact on changing the corporate culture. When it is implemented with lip service and desire for a "quick fix," it is doomed to fail like other initiatives of its kind.

CHAPTER FIFTEEN

PUTTING IT OUT THERE—ON THE NET

"Getting information off the Internet is like taking a drink from a fire hydrant."

—MITCHELL KAPOR, FOUNDER OF LOTUS DEVELOPMENT CORP.

IN THE PREVIOUS CHAPTER, I described the concept of putting your corporate values, commitments, and missions out for people to see them. What better way to do this then over the Internet? During my quest for the best service providers, I went to the website of every one of the companies I portrayed to see what they had to say about themselves. Not surprisingly, each of these companies stated clearly on the World Wide Web what they were all about, what they believe in. I thought it would be interesting to review these company websites now.

Before we begin, I want to point out that this is not a critique of any individual company's website design or appeal to me. Websites are becoming more and more e-commerce–focused, so the emphasis on most websites is a combination of selling products and services or providing customer service once the sale is made. Each of these sites is designed differently, depending upon the objective of the site itself. Some I personally like better than others.

What I am interested in sharing with you, however, is the stated commitment that each of these companies is making to what is valuable to them, their values. By seeing these values in print, we can assess whether these companies live by these same values in their daily service to their customers. Assuming that they do, we can only assume that this plays at least a part in the ways in which they separate themselves from the others in their industries. I also want to provide some examples of ways in which your company might incorporate your value system into your website.

L.L.BEAN

Since I began my quest with L.L.Bean, I'll start with a look at its website. It can be found at www.llbean.com. Notice that at the top of the page, as well as again on the home page, you find the link to "100% Guaranteed." Clicking on this sends you to this statement:

> From kayaks to slippers, fly rods to sweaters, everything we sell at L.L.Bean is backed by the same rock-solid guarantee of satisfaction. It's been that way since our founder sold his very first pair of Bean Boots in 1912. Today we're proud to continue the tradition—by offering quality products and standing behind them. Of course, we want you to be the final judge of quality. If you're not satisfied with your purchase, we'll replace it or give you your money back. It's that simple.

L.L.Bean doesn't hesitate to put its commitment out there. It is what has driven the company since its inception. Satisfaction guaranteed.

ST. JUDE CHILDREN'S RESEARCH CENTER

At its website, www.stjude.org, you'll see at the top of the home page the statement "Saving Children." That is what the center does and what each employee at St. Jude will tell you he or she does. They don't each touch a child; many there can do their daily jobs and never even see a patient. But each one knows that his or her individual job contributes toward saving the life of a child. During the many times that I have had the privilege of speaking to employees and volunteers for ALSAC (the fund-raising organization for St. Jude) and St. Jude, I have always noticed the signs and banners that are displayed throughout the hospital. Each banner may have its own theme, but all of them will have one saying in common, somewhere on them: "Saving children's lives." They know what they do, and put it out there for people to see.

CHICK-FIL-A

At www.chick-fil-a.com, you will find a prominent link to a separate website for the Truett Cathy story. That link tells you the entire story of Chick-fil-A and its principles. It opens like this:

> Armed with a keen business sense, a work ethic forged during the Depression, and a personal and business philosophy based on biblical principles, Truett Cathy took a tiny Atlanta diner, originally called the Dwarf Grill, and transformed it into Chick-fil-A, the nation's second largest quick-service chicken restaurant chain with nearly $1.75 billion in sales in 2004 and currently more than 1,200 locations. His tremendous business success allowed Truett to pursue other passions—most notably his interest in the development of young people.

Note the fact that the values and principles of the founder require an entire website to contain.

THE RITZ-CARLTON

At www.ritzcarlton.com, a link will take you to the Leadership Center, where the mission is described like this:

> Launched in 2000, The Ritz-Carlton Leadership Center has welcomed thousands of senior executives, managers and line staff from very diverse industries such as Automotive, Finance, Food Services, Healthcare, Human Resources, Retail and Transportation. The Leadership Center has flourished as a resource center for leading organizations interested in benchmarking many of the business practices that led to our becoming a two-time recipient of the Malcolm Baldrige National Quality Award.
>
> The services of The Ritz-Carlton Leadership Center are ideal if your organization is looking to create sustainable change, out-perform the competition and increase employee and customer loyalty. The knowledge and information participants receive transcend all industries and levels of leadership."

You'll also find a link to the "Gold Standard," which will take you to the motto, credo, steps of service, basics, and promises of The Ritz-Carlton. This is a company that is proud enough of the way it does business that it offers it out to any company, whether a competitor or not, to emulate. How many companies do you know that will take their most valuable asset and make it available to others?

MRS. FIELDS

The website www.mrsfields.com has been going through some changes. The new version is now up and running, but it calls the company "Mrs. Fields Gifts, Inc." In candor and with all due respect to the company, I personally feel that it has lost a lot of its appeal and mystique since Debbi Fields sold her stake in the business and now is more of a figurehead for the company than an actual leader of it. I sense that much of the passion has been removed. In the past, the personality of Debbi Fields was more prevalent in the website and advertising. While the company still creates a wonderful product and commands a large share of its market, the Debbi Fields impact has been diluted over the recent years. In my opinion, this is missed.

NORDSTROM

Like most retail stores, the Nordstrom website at www.nordstrom .com emphasizes sales. A look inside the site, however, finds a focus on its family of employees, opening with this statement:

> Nordstrom began as a shoe store in Seattle, Washington in 1901. Today, we are one of the largest independently-owned fashion specialty stores in the nation. Our founder, John W. Nordstrom, believed in a simple philosophy: Listen to the customer. Provide them with what they want. Appreciate the fact they came to your store, and do everything within your power to ensure that they're satisfied when they leave.

Additionally, you find quotes from employees, which include references to their pride in the company, their ability to operate independently, and their focus on creating a unique and memorable customer experience.

FEDEX

Go to www.fedex.com, and you'll quickly be introduced to the commitment of the company's mission of 100 percent successful package delivery. Once again, the commerce of the site, which focuses primarily on supporting customers with packages sent out, does not preclude presenting the clearly stated values and vision of the company or the pride in its heritage.

THE BADDOUR CENTER

There are challenges found elsewhere throughout this book, so I thought I would issue another one here. If you go to www .baddour.org, click on the "Miracles" link and don't feel a rush of serotonin, you will need to be examined by your physician. This entire website is about kindness, and you will not be able to miss it when you visit the site.

CHAPTER SIXTEEN

CONCLUSIONS

"*Reasoning draws a conclusion, but does not make the conclusion certain, unless the mind discovers it by the path of experience.*"
—ROGER BACON

FOR THE PURPOSES OF THIS BOOK, my quest for the best in service is over. However, my personal quest is definitely not over. I hope it stays perpetual.

I have paid closer attention to service of all types since I began to write this book. I have observed service in government, retail, manufacturing, nonprofits—you name it. I have studied providers and users of the services that these groups provide. I have developed an unquenched thirst for what makes the difference in service today. I realize, and accept, that my views and opinions are not popular with proponents of Six Sigma, the Excellence Model, ISO 9001, and other fads. Some cannot accept my theory that it is not process but people in service that make *all* the difference, simply because it is too simple. I'm okay with that.

What I'm not okay with, however, is the indifference that I observe within companies that have spent literally millions of dollars on systems looking to fix the indifference in their customer service.

One of the single most frequent complaints that I hear has

to do with the use of automated answering attendants and integrated voice responders in customer service. From a service provider's standpoint, these devices are efficient, cost-effective, reliable, and flexible. However, customers don't want to have these cold, impersonal devices be the line of communication when there is a problem.

Just as vocal are the customers who do not want to talk to either incoherent or indistinguishable live reps. To get a good conversation started about customer service, just mention a problem you had recently with not being able to understand a server at a fast-food restaurant, or a clerk at a retail store.

So people are not happy when the systems work, like in the first example of automation, and they're not happy when the personal touch part doesn't work, as in the second example. If the only solution is perfection, where everybody is happy with the service they get all the time, we can forget it. No company is ever going to achieve that.

I have reached some conclusions during my journey, and they are listed below. They may not be all-inclusive, but they are based on my observations, and I feel strongly about each one. They are listed in no particular order or significance; they contribute equally to this malaise of service that I am experiencing in an economy that has service at its core. They are conclusions that bother me as I write them. They are as follows.

EVERY BUSINESS HAS TO PROVIDE SERVICE

The logical way to keep customers happy is to not have any customer service problems. I accept this. If I offer something that has zero defects and zero problems, customer service is pretty simple. Likewise, if I offer a product or service and don't sell any of it at all, I have no service issues. The problem with either of these examples is that neither is attainable for very long. Sooner or later, my product or service is going to have a problem of some sort. Similarly, I'm not going to stay in business long without sales. Therefore, there is no possibility of my not offering some kind of service. It is a requirement of any business. Every company or service provider has a customer service department, even if it is not "labeled" that way. Does your dentist's office have a customer service department? It does when you call for directions. What about your hair stylist? Yes, when he or she sets your appointment and takes your money. Does your attorney? Yes, each time you get a bill. Each of these is a function of service. Every contact is service. There is no service provided that does not include customer service of some sort. None. Everything that is done for, or on behalf of, someone else includes service.

PERFECTION IS IMPOSSIBLE; PROBLEMS MUST BE ANTICIPATED

I have observed many companies that feel that the solution to customer service is the elimination of defects or problems. This is a worthy goal, but perfection is not attainable. Companies may get close, but they'll never be perfect. FedEx pursues perfection, but it also realizes that it is not in its grasp, and it works as hard on fixing the inevitable errors as it does on the perfection. Not working hard on the error part is what is wrong with many companies today. They simply overlook the problem part of their business when the fix is right in front of them! They could assess what kind of problems happen most frequently and decide what is the best way to deal with them if they can't be eliminated.

For example, my cable company is never going to be perfect. Things are always going to go wrong. It could easily calculate how many problems it has each month, overlay how many people are needed to support those problems, and configure support accordingly. Instead, it calculates how much it makes on each subscriber, throws a support number at that top number, and tries to make sure there is something left after the subtraction. The company's problems are not going to go away! However, it is more worried about the bottom line than it is about the customer service provided. Do you know anybody who claims they get good service from their cable company?

COMPANIES HIRE FOR SKILLS, NOT ATTITUDE

I am more convinced than ever that there are people with good attitudes looking for employment opportunities. I am just as convinced that companies looking for employees consider attitude to be unimportant, simply a phrase on their job application form. If this is not the case, there must be some real flaws in the attitude-screening process.

How much time are companies taking to screen potential employees' attitudes? My answer has got to be "not enough." I hope that most applicants are smart enough to answer the "attitude" questions correctly. I also would hope that they have enough sense to provide only references who will say nice things about them. The only way to assess someone's attitude is to spend some time with him or her, get to know the person. Companies don't have time for that today; they'd rather hire someone with the right skills, since this can be assessed much more easily. What they are missing is the costs associated with hiring the wrong people, regardless of their skills, and then having to replace them. These companies appear to be doing the same tired dance over and over, looking for the combination of skill and attitude in the wrong order.

SOME PEOPLE CAN'T BE FIXED

There are some people who simply are not going to come around and develop an attitude of courtesy and respect. It is not in them, and never will be. I'm not saying that people are not *all* deserving of courtesy and kindness. I am saying, however, that not everyone is willing to *offer* these same traits. Due to their environment, upbringing, education, or perhaps just their stubbornness, there are some who are simply not going to go to the trouble to use common courtesy and politeness. There are prejudices that are not going to be corrected, anger that is not going to be resolved, and attitudes that will never be adjusted. I wish I could be proven wrong here, but I am skeptical of our ability to create drastic change in the attitudes of people.

THE LAW OF ATTRACTION WORKS

For many years, I have believed in the power of visualization and positive thinking. I believe that we are what we think, and that energy attracts like energy.

What I didn't realize until I started work on this book is how clearly apparent it is that companies attract a certain kind of employee and that these employees attract a certain type of customer. Observe patrons at restaurants and shoppers at retail stores and shops. Pay attention to the employees, and compare them to their regular customers. You will see striking similarities between the two. You will also see strong similarities when you look at the people doing the hiring and providing the leadership of these employees, who are attracting the customers. I have been observing this from the service angle for some time, and I have not seen it fail.

SOME COMPANIES SHOULD NOT BE IN BUSINESS

I am believer in free enterprise and the capitalist form of society. I am also an entrepreneur and small business advocate. I just as strongly believe that there are many businesses that should not be in existence, that serve no purpose for their existence.

These companies hire otherwise unemployable individuals, but instead of mentoring them or teaching them to be better with both their skills and attitudes, they put them out into customer contact with instructions to perform menial tasks and nothing more. There is no pride, no dignity in the job, simply process. Without challenges, pride, contributions to decisions, and leadership, these employees find themselves with idle minds and zero interest in the jobs they do and the services they provide. They are there, period. They are paid to be there, period.

In my opinion, these companies are useless and serve no good. They *could* serve some good if their principals and owners would contribute to their employees' growth by providing concern for their futures, such as that provided by Chick-fil-A. Absent these concerns, however, they serve no good other than to serve coffee and sandwiches. That is not enough.

OUR PUBLIC EDUCATIONAL SYSTEM IS FAILING US

I am sick of paying to be served by ignorance. I'm not talking about attitudes here; I am speaking of service provided by people who are completely incapable of communication because of their lack of basic education. In our society, with the emphasis on service being required by virtually every company, I find this to be absolutely unacceptable. Basic reading and communication skills must be required in our educational systems; they are not.

FAMILIES ARE THE BEST TEACHERS

I would like to see a new interviewing process that includes bringing in the parents of prospective employees for interviews. I have long been a proponent of the apple not falling far from the tree. True, I have seen good kids come from bad parents, but more often I have seen good kids come from parents with values. It is rare that troubled kids come from families with strong core values. It's not unusual to have kids in trouble, but it is less likely to have troubled kids. There is a difference.

During the research for this book, I got a strong dose of "today's kids" being the problem. I heard everything from education to upbringing, from being spoiled to being ingrates. For some, it is all about the kids. I tend to prefer the Nordstrom philosophy, that the best trainer of employees is their parents. I am disgusted at the number of irresponsible parents who are setting such poor examples for many young people. I am just as frustrated with the cavalier attitudes of other family leaders when it comes to complete lack of respect for adults, possessions, and feelings of others that are being taught in too many homes.

HR FEARS ARE CONTROLLING HOW EXECUTIVES HANDLE PROBLEM EMPLOYEES

One of the common issues that I heard discussed during my research was the difficulty that many executives sense when it comes to making changes once an individual has been hired. Company leaders expressed a virtual consensus when asked whether they moved quickly when mistakes were made in hiring with regard to attitudes. They all agreed that swift correction should be made. The leaders of the larger firms, however, admitted concern that their ability to act quickly enough was restricted. Fears of lawsuits and monetary awards cause these executives to be more than cautious in many circumstances, so they feel compelled to observe helplessly as bad attitudes flow through their organizations. I find that smaller companies are more aggressive in their corrective action regarding poor attitudes. This may explain why I also find exceptional service philosophies in smaller companies rather than in larger ones.

VALUES MAKE THE DIFFERENCE

This is the strongest conclusion I have reached; it is the core statement of this book. Whether from the founders of the organization or the current leadership of the company, I am convinced of the fact that values play the most significant role in determining how customers and employees are treated in any organization. Notice that I didn't say, "a" significant role. I said, "the" significant role. I challenge anyone to show me otherwise.

Just as in families, there are beliefs in companies that are transparent to employees and customers alike. Some have shallow, limited values; others thrive in deep, constant abiding faith in their values. In either case, the levels of commitment to these respective values are clear in either their presence or absence. From meetings to websites, from action to talk, they are either there or not.

Many of you may recognize the absence of any type of values in your own companies. I hope that you will just as quickly review the impact of these values in your company and put beliefs in dignity, respect, courtesy, and kindness in place.

SOME TRUE STORIES

DURING THE COURSE of preparing this book, I heard numerous stories from colleagues, friends, and listeners to my radio show *Talk About Service*, to add to my personal experiences and observations. While the majority of the stories I was told were negative, there were also many positive ones as well. I thought it might be good to compile some of these, share them with you, and discuss why they were handled correctly if they are positive, and if they are not, how they might be better handled and whether a kindness revolution could have helped.

All of these stories are true. Some will have you shaking your head as to how they can happen, but you will recognize some of these as being similar to experiences you have personally had. Unfortunately for the poor examples, this is their advertising. This is what their customers are talking about. This is how they are seen in the market.

As you read these stories, ask yourself the following questions: How would my company handle this situation? Could this be happening in my firm? How can we avoid this (if the example is bad)? How can we match this (if the example is good)?

Let's see how service is being offered today.

From listener Ben: "I was invited by a friend to join him for a drink at a new restaurant in town. As I walked into the bar, I noticed the bottles on the wall of the bar. I sat down and ordered a particular brand of whiskey, eight-year-old Old Charter with water. The waitress politely said, 'we don't have Charter eight, but we have ten-year-old Charter.' I casually mentioned to the waitress that I prefer eight-year-old Charter, but I accepted the drink and continued to talk to my buddy. A few minutes after my drink was served, another gentleman came out with a drink in his hand. He asked who had ordered the eight-year-old Charter and water and I said, 'I did.' He set the drink down, said the first drink was on him, and explained that the new drink was eight-year-old Charter and that they would have it from now on.

Obviously, I was impressed. I asked him where he got the eight-year-old Charter and he explained that he was the manager and had sent someone to the liquor store to get a bottle.

What we can learn from this: Ben was "wowed." After he told this story on the air, I asked Ben how often he had told others about this. "All the time," was his response. I asked him if he went back to this restaurant. "Same answer," was his reply. This is advertising for this restaurant that can't be purchased and cost about ten minutes of time and a good decision by a manager. In addition, this manager is setting an example for the other restaurant employees of going out of the way to provide outstanding customer service.

Here's one that's not so good.

A personal experience: Listeners to my radio show and speeches know that I don't like to fly because of the current level of customer service offered by most airlines.

I recently changed flights in Minneapolis on my way to speak in Seattle. The flight was a three-hour affair, and the plane was packed. I discovered that I was in the middle seat in the very back row of the plane.

After making my way to the back of the plane, I saw that the man in the window seat was a very large person. Not obese, simply a very large man. His knees were literally forced into the seats in front of him and he had to lift the arm rest to fit into his seat—and mine. I had less than half of my seat to fit into.

I somehow got into the seat for take off and, following the appropriate signals from the pilot that it was all right to move around the plane, I got out and stood in the rear of the airplane. I was quickly greeted by a cranky flight attendant who told me curtly to "take a seat."

After politely explaining my dilemma, the attendant proceeded to give me a five or ten minute lecture regarding what I "should have done" for her to help me. When I asked what that help would have been, she said "I would have put you on a later flight."

What we can learn from this: When customers have a problem, they are not interested in "what they should have done." What they *are* interested in, however, is a solution to their problem. In this instance, I would have been happy with a little empathy and delighted in an attempt to solve the problem, such as checking in the bulkhead seats to see if someone would change seats (remember, the gentleman next to me was as uncomfortable as I was). If the airline had encouraged an atmosphere such as that at St. Jude, where each employee felt proud to be part of the company and internalized the company's mission of serving its customers, I might at least have gotten a more polite, sympathetic response. Instead, what I got was indifference. What the airline got was negative advertising that it didn't buy.

From listener Pat: "Ed, I was at a floral shop ordering some flowers this week. A man behind the counter was on the phone with a customer. When he hung up, he turned to the lady helping me, rolled his eyes, and said of the customer he was speaking to, 'That bitch is crazy!'

"This made me very uncomfortable and I wonder what they will say about ME when I leave! I don't think I'll go back there."

What we can learn from this: It is simply never good to comment on the behavior of customers or your opinion of them. Whether it is on the phone, in conversation, or e-mails, nothing should be said of a customer that you wouldn't want him or her to hear. Remember this: Praise in public and criticize in private. Don't let negative comments be heard, period. An employee in a store that talked about customer service every day, like they do at The Ritz-Carlton, would never have behaved this way.

An e-mail from listener Jamie: "Ed, I have a doozie of a bad one for you!

"My ex–family physician's office is also a minor medical. I had an appointment for 2:00 p.m. I went to the office, signed in at 1:40, and told them I had an appointment (they want you to let them know whether you have an appointment or if you are a walk-in).

"The receptionist looked at me and said, 'The doctors have been busy with walk-ins all day and won't be seeing any more patients until after 3:00.'

> *Me:* "But I have an APPOINTMENT at 2:00."
> *Receptionist:* "Sorry, but they won't resume seeing patients until 3:00."

Me: "And will those people with appointments be taken
in first at 3:00?"
Receptionist: *shrug* "I don't know," and she turned
around and walked away.

"Needless to say I did exactly the same thing and found myself a new physician."

What we can learn from this: The medical profession gets
hit as hard as any profession or industry when it comes to customer service. Customers, in this case patients, are tired of making apparently meaningless appointments. All businesses can
learn from this.

When asking customers to work around *your* schedule, provide the courtesy of notice when a delay is going to occur. If
businesses are not aware of the importance of this, it could cost
them business. If the receptionist had been encouraged and empowered to solve customer (patient) dilemmas like the employees at Nordstrom are, the outcome might have been different.

Another personal experience: I was recently recommended a
lawn maintenance company by my youngest son, who owns a
landscape company. I contacted the maintenance company to
schedule a meeting to get a quote for "spring cleaning" for my
lawn. I wanted to do business with this company!

I didn't get a call back for a couple of days. When I did get
the call, it was full of apologies for the delay in calling me. The
meeting was scheduled and then moved back at the last minute
by the owner of the maintenance company. I was told that I
would get a quote the next day. Three days later, I got the quote
by phone and told the company, "Let's go." I was told that the
work would be done two days later.

Five days later, after numerous calls inquiring as to when the
work would be done, I had not received a call. No concern, no

follow-up, no explanations or rescheduling. The next call I made was to fire the lawn company.

What we can learn from this: One of the most frequent complaints I hear from customers regards lack of follow-up. This includes not following up on scheduled visits, not keeping customers informed of open service problems, and not getting call backs. A little effort on keeping customers informed can go a tremendously long way toward keeping customers. A company committed from the top down to "totally reliable" service, such as FedEx, which keeps the lines of communication open to the extent of letting customers track the progress of its service, would not have wound up in this situation, which, in my case, caused the company to lose a new customer.

The stories are never ending. These are just a few of the literally hundreds I have heard. Companies of all sizes should be reminded again that your customers are talking about their experiences in dealing with you. It can be the best—or worst—advertising you can get. Think about how a kindness revolution in your company might help your employees to be the kind of representatives you want advertising your services.

INDEX